Praise for

HOMEWORK

"Leadership is messy, complicated, and difficult. And that's on the good days. This helpful book shines interdisciplinary wisdom onto the building blocks of leadership."
MICHAEL BUNGAY STANIER, bestselling author of *The Coaching Habit* and *How to Begin*

"Deena Chochinov has written a unique, practical, and groundbreaking book that draws on her multiple roles and expertise—as a family therapist, systems consultant to organizations, and a family business advisor. The book shows how these three lenses can work together to help complex family enterprises. It is rich and full of stories that highlight how a family can work through a dilemma. She begins with a view of leadership and expands this to show how leadership takes on special complexity in business families, and how leadership must focus on the whole systems of business, family, and individual working in harmony."
DENNIS JAFFE, Senior Research Fellow, BanyanGlobal Family Business Advisors

"In her remarkably accessible book *HomeWork*, Deena Chochinov provides both a vision and a roadmap for the pivots and processes of systemic change through clear, step-by-step, practical applications. The book doesn't just hold the prescription, but rather supports the leader's intrinsic ability to learn and grow. It's possible to like the company you keep."

JAY LAPPIN, MSW, LCSW, Minuchin Center for the Family

"This thoughtful, practical book uniquely illuminates the ways our professional skills can also support a more harmonious home life—and vice versa. I can't wait to put its tools to work on both fronts."

ALEXANDRA SAMUEL, co-author of *Remote, Inc.: How to Thrive at Work...Wherever You Are*

"Deena Chochinov writes in service of her reader, balancing wisdom with application. She successfully bridges the why with the how, supported by research and animated by relatable stories. Few leadership books wed 'being' and 'doing' so beautifully. Whether you are a leader of your family, a leader of an organization, or navigating the complexity of leadership in your family enterprise, you'll want to develop the traits and implement the practices here so you can grow and flourish in both your home and work domains."

RUTH E. STEVERLYNCK, LL.B (Hons), FEA, Family Firm Institute Fellow

"This book is so insightful and relevant that I felt Deena Chochinov knew just what leadership guidance I needed. She intuits what it takes to be a great leader, and a great human. I love this book. Every entrepreneur should run to buy this book and absorb its powerful lessons."

SHERRY DEUTSCHMANN, founder and CEO, BrainTrust

"*HomeWork* is an essential read! Deena Chochinov's expertise is very much evident through her clear, concise, accessible, and actionable approach. This book is incredibly timely, and highly recommended for any organization struggling to understand what matters most these days. I loved her emphasis on systems thinking versus hoping for a single 'magic bean' to make everything better. The inclusion of eight interpersonal/interactive qualities will truly add value to any organization!"

JAN JOHNSON, VP Workplace Strategy at Allsteel

"A user's guide to leadership, presented at a time when all the boundaries between office and home have evaporated. *HomeWork* gives us the opportunity to show up in both places as the same person—ourselves."

AYSE BIRSEL, industrial designer and author of *Design the Life You Love*

HOME
WORK

HOME

How to Be a Leader in the Boardroom and the Living Room

WORK

DEENA CHOCHINOV

PAGE TWO

Cataloguing in publication information is available from Library and Archives Canada.
ISBN 978-1-77458-210-7 (paperback)
ISBN 978-1-77458-211-4 (ebook)

Page Two
pagetwo.com

Edited by Amanda Lewis
Copyedited by Jonathan Dore
Cover and interior design by Jennifer Lum

deenachochinov.com

To my parents, Earl and Ethel Chochinov,

for their unceasing commitment, support, and love.

Thank you for making the ambient soundtrack of my

life one of joyful curiosity and endless possibility.

KNOW ALL THE THEORIES,
MASTER ALL THE TECHNIQUES,
BUT AS YOU TOUCH A HUMAN
SOUL BE JUST ANOTHER
HUMAN SOUL.

CARL JUNG

CONTENTS

INTRODUCTION
The Case for Whole and Integrated Leadership

WHAT IS THIS BOOK AND WHY IS IT DIFFERENT?

There are a lot of great books out there on leadership. And most of those books focus on making decisions, inspiring and engaging teams, managing change, and beating the competition.

There are also a lot of books about people—about psychology, personal self-help, professional development, and the many, many ways to understand and manage the complex dynamics in all our different relationships.

But this book is different.

For the past three decades, I have been practicing in three professional fields that are seldom mentioned in the same sentence, but which together give me a unique perspective on leadership and its extraordinary potential. I'm an expert in family therapy, organizational development (OD) consulting, and family business advising. What are these three fields made of?

Family therapy is a psychological practice that studies and treats families as whole systems of interrelated parts. It concentrates on the structures and processes that make families function, the interpersonal patterns of interacting, and the acceptance of how families can change, grow, and ultimately thrive. Here, a "systems approach" is critical for understanding families and stewarding interventions in ways that acknowledge that all families—without exception—can be best understood as "dynamic systems." In this therapeutic methodology, we look at the family as a living system with all of its idiosyncrasies, as well as the particular characteristics each member brings to that constellation of relationships. These include, but are not limited to, proximity and distance, communication patterns, generational hierarchies, and healthy boundaries. A family-systems approach factors in various and changing roles and identities, and how members see themselves as either a part of, or apart from, the family as a whole.

In my clinical work with families, couples, and individuals, I always consider the relational systems they came from, the ones they inhabit now, and how these systems affect their behaviors, relationships, and general well-being. These clients offer me their time and trust as they navigate the various territories of their lives, despite the barriers in their paths. They maneuver the precarious emotional landscapes of suppression, repression, and depression—the experience of being held down, holding something down, or simply *feeling* down. They seek and keep healthy relationships or rekindle connection with a spouse after it's been tested or threatened. They feel disquiet about managing too many roles—partner, parent, professional, sibling, adult child—when there's not enough time, money, or energy to do this, regardless of intention or desire. They want to lead a life with dignity and integrity, recognizing those moments of grace and wonder in the face of turmoil and tension.

Organizational development consulting is the study and practice of effecting organizational change so that the culture and climate can support and engage the people who work in it. Through this critical lens, I see every company as an "organization" of people, a living system of interconnected parts that, all together, can contribute to the success or failure of the business they are in and the services they provide to their customers, clients, and stakeholders. OD consultants mostly center our work on the people who are charged with creating a healthy, high-performance culture and leading their organizations with purpose and passion. We support them to make the big decisions, instigate change (hopefully for the better), and bring their teams along to embrace new ideas and implement winning solutions. But for any of these interventions to work, we need to consider the people in the system—their expectations, personality styles, motivations, barriers, priorities, talents, and skills—and the relationships between those people in the workplace. As with family systems, if we understand the functional and dysfunctional dynamics in the different parts of the organizational system, we can help to create change that is healthy, effective, and lasting.

My OD consulting clients are the leaders and senior teams of corporations, social enterprises, public and not-for-profit organizations, as well as entrepreneurs and managers. They all seem to be consumed with similar needs and concerns that require an objective listener. They are agents of change who are obsessed with creating healthy, sustainable, and progressive corporate cultures. They care deeply about keeping their employees, customers, suppliers, and partners engaged, loyal, and satisfied. They worry about power, money, and success, and they work hard to manage their relationships at work and at home so they don't end up burning out after all the effort and time they put into getting to that place of leadership.

Family business advising is the third field of practice in which I work, one that provides an unparalleled example of where the dynamic systems of home and work come together. Family businesses (also known as family enterprises) have a significant impact on the economies of many countries around the globe. They encompass two-thirds of businesses worldwide with an annual global GDP of 70–90 percent, and provide up to 80 percent of jobs in the majority of countries.[1] In Canada, family-owned enterprises generate almost half of the nation's private sector GDP, account for 63 percent of all private sector businesses, and generate 47 percent of that sector's employment.[2] In the United States, family businesses account for 50 percent of the GDP and are responsible for 60 percent of the nation's employment and 78 percent of new jobs created.[3] Because this sector is such an economic and social force, there is a growing field of practice and research focusing on family-enterprise ownership, business practices, and interpersonal dynamics.

As you've likely guessed from the previous paragraphs, family businesses can also be effectively understood through the lens of systems theory. By definition (and moniker), they are the *literal* marriages of "family" and "business," two separate but connected systems, where "home" and "work" need to functionally coexist. You might suspect—especially if you recall stories from friends who are involved in family businesses—that on good days they are in happy harmony, but on the bad ones, they can be on a collision course of conflict. And you'd be right.

I think of the family business as a kind of crucible where the peaks and valleys of the emotional, the operational, the aspirational, and the strategic elements of this very complex system of relationships come together. But although family businesses are where the overlap between home and work may seem the most overt, they—like all businesses—have their own unique set of cultural norms, values and behavioral patterns, rituals and flashpoints, which must all be understood and managed.

Because their home and work worlds are so inextricably tied, my family-enterprise clients often need support in navigating how to lead effectively, communicate clearly, and manage conflict with kindness; how to develop strategies, processes, and structures that allow the business to grow and succeed and the family to stay united and strong; how to create a family culture of generosity and purpose; and how to prepare the rising generations to lead the enterprise, ensuring its continuity over time. These families want to maintain and grow their relational health so that they can increase their societal impact and enjoy their financial wealth.

WHY IS THIS IMPORTANT?

Throughout the last decade of my career, it became increasingly clear to me that much of what I do at the micro-level—counseling individuals, couples, and families—had a significant overlap or crossover with what I did at the macro-level—consulting with companies, organizations, and nonprofits, and coaching their leaders and senior teams. (Sometimes I think of my work as "helping small struggling families" and "helping large struggling families.") Once I added in the expertise I had developed working in the specialized field of family-enterprise advising, the opportunity of sharing my practice—and this book—became clear.

I've learned that there are not-so-hidden connections between leadership in the boardroom and leadership in the living room. So many of the qualities and actions my counseling clients practice at home (perhaps unwittingly) resemble those embraced by my coaching and consulting clients in their roles at work. This realization challenged my old notion of a dichotomous split or separation between our work and home selves; instead, I have a more nuanced understanding of our many overlaps and alignments between the different systems.

True leadership requires the full integration of our professional and personal selves so that we show up as whole, in both places. Somehow, we got the message that we're required to present differently in the two territories we spend most of our lives in—home and work—that to be successful we require a split in our roles and therefore in our selves. But we aren't a chest of drawers with different compartments to hold distinctly separate aspects of who we are and what we do. This dual-identity ethos is forced on us by years of socialization, but it's a myth—and a dangerous one at that.

Whole and integrated leadership is the antidote. Managing separate identities not only doesn't serve us, it derails our ability to be gifted, skillful leaders in all the domains we inhabit. The cost of buying into the separation-of-selves philosophy leads to internal chaos and even fragmentation, a state of dividing into pieces and feeling like we're broken apart. The benefits of making a paradigm shift to holistic leadership are psychological congruence and stability, and the full integration of our undivided, messy, textured, complex, and beautifully appointed selves. We can have success at work and harmony at home—being the exact same person.

Sure, we make different decisions at work and at home, but the qualities of holistic leadership influence how we make those decisions in both places. After all, leadership isn't just about what you do, it's about how you show up.

This book is a kind of "user's guide" of the most useful, helpful, and repeatable leadership lessons, learnings, best practices, and insights from the family domain and the organizational world—from "home" and "work." It offers you tips for how to be successful in both spheres.

And that's how the book you are holding was born, with an obvious title: *HomeWork*.

HOW THIS BOOK IS ORGANIZED

Because being and doing are interdependent elements of successful leadership, I have developed a roadmap that brings together both the holistic qualities of *how* a leader behaves and the thoughtful actions of *what* a leader does. I believe this process of integration is the work all leaders need to do, so consider this your call to action.

Part 1: Qualities of Leadership

First, there's the "*how.*"

I've identified certain patterns of behavior that are unmistakable indicators of leadership success or failure. When they show up with these behaviors, leaders attain a vitality and "flow" with their followers. When these qualities are missing, their leadership challenges multiply, worsen, and become more entrenched.

A successful leader's way of being is just as important as what they are doing.

Part 1 of the book offers you the eight essential qualities that wholly integrated leaders need to thrive, regardless of the system they live and work within. I'll describe the elements of each quality, and offer a collection of tools and techniques you can use to cultivate and practice each quality.

A successful leader's way of being is just as important as what they are doing.

Part 2: Leadership Lessons

Then there's the "*what.*"

What must leaders actually do every day to make a difference? What actions do they take to guide their teams, stay on track, and achieve results? I've spent years listening to my clients describe what works and what doesn't, and again I've found recurring themes from their experiences as executives, parents, and partners.

In Part 2 of the book, I translate these themes into eight leadership lessons-in-action, offering you a clear roadmap to create healthy, effective, and engaged systems; set a strategic path forward; and get things done.

Everyone enjoys reading stories, and good stories help us empathize with others and take their challenges to heart. So these HomeWork lessons are gleaned from stories, or case studies, as I'll be referring to them. These case studies will move between the three domains described above (family, business, and family enterprise), highlighting where they are similar and where they are different, but mostly what they can, together, teach us about effective leadership. Between each set of case studies, I will provide a short "*Crossover*" moment, offering highlights and clues to what to look out for. This will help you focus on the patterns in each case study, and prompt you to compare it to the challenges and opportunities that you see in your own life.

At the end of each lesson, I'll give *you* some homework! Taking the form of structured, guided self-reflections and actionable exercises, this homework will serve not only you, but also the people around you—either at work or at home. There will be many times when you can engage your teams, partners, and kids to do these self-reflections together, and, truth be told, doing these as a small group may yield the most effective results.

In the end, I don't want you to walk away from this book with just a set of memorable anecdotes about home and work. I want you to take away a new systemic lens on leadership where we bring our whole selves to that role at work and at home. Being "in charge" is a complicated and demanding business. And let's face it, even if you are the most collaborative and inclusive servant-leader to your family or your company, you're still ultimately responsible for creating the circumstances for their well-being and success. They are looking to you for support, guidance, and sustenance. Being true to them means manifesting the qualities of holistic leadership as you escort them into action.

WHY THIS BOOK, NOW?

People have been talking about the home/work dichotomy since we separated the homes we live in and the places where we work into two distinct spaces. You hear it all the time: "I really need to keep my home life and my work life separate" or "I am vowing to never check email after 9 pm." For leaders whose breadth and depth of responsibilities often necessitate an "always on" posture, the demands can be crushing. Sometimes this struggle shows up in our tools: "Honestly, I have two phones and it's not really helping at all," and a lot of the time, the demands are nonsensical: "The fact that my boss wants me to never check on my babysitter while I'm at work is preposterous and unrealistic."

Unfortunately, there are many leaders who—at least, judged by what they say—have completely given up. They tell me, "I have no work-life balance, and I really don't care to. I think that whole thing is a myth anyway." Other leaders are desperately trying *not* to completely give up: "I can only exercise in the early mornings—not because I want to, but because as soon as the workday starts, it's impossible for me to take any time for myself." Throw in career ambitions and anxiety, increasing responsibility and decreasing resources, the perpetual threat of job insecurity, and the constant pressure from staff, stakeholders, society, and social media to succeed, and you can see how the challenge of work-life balance is coming to a crisis point.

And then, well, there *was* an actual crisis. As I write this sentence, we are two years into the COVID-19 pandemic (December 2021), and beyond all the tragedy and loss, anyone lucky enough to have a job—or to have employees and hopes to create jobs—has had the work-life conundrum turned on its head . . . in lots of ways, but particularly in one: work-from-home, or WFH. The pandemic, in many parts of the world, has ushered in a new and frankly epochal collapse of home and work—literally moving the "doing of the work" into the home by necessity rather than choice. Along with navigating the many demands and activities in the home—childrearing, cooking, cleaning, scheduling, teaching, nourishing, encouraging, and entertaining, to name a handful—now our home lives are supposed to magically coexist with our work lives, and vice versa. This seems, and feels, impossible, and for many of us who have tried, the challenges have been overwhelming.

Can we find ways through this omnipresent challenge, the tests of which feel unprecedented? I believe we can, through learning from the dynamics of family and organizational systems. In this book, I'll offer you a roadmap, a toolkit, and a repeatable way to work with your team and family to keep things together, and even thrive.

PART
ONE

HOW TO BE A LEADER

The 8 Leadership
Qualities and the
Tools and Techniques
to Cultivate Them

THERE IS A boldness born from a leader's express intention to learn, to create, and to accomplish something. However they choose to define achievement, leaders have a deliberate and greater-than-average drive to succeed. From the family business owners who feel compelled to create a legacy over generations, to the managers who offer their staff every chance to develop their skills and talents, to the parents who nurture their children's creativity into being, leaders take all kinds of action to open doors, present opportunities, offer inspiration, and get results. But what are the qualities that propel leaders to act?

During my years in practice, certain leaders have stood out for their exceptional ways of being. They are noticeable by virtue of their authenticity, impact... and, well, goodness. Both in action and *inter*action at home and at work, these executives, managers, parents, and spouses embody qualities that contribute to the health and success of their family and organizational systems.

Although not exactly magical, they definitely practice a kind of grounded alchemy that is able to inspire others, transform relationships, and create profound and positive results regardless of the context or circumstance. This is quite a feat, considering that these leaders are working at least one of the two hardest jobs in the world: managing people at work and raising kids at home. Let's add sustaining a healthy romantic partnership to that list too!

The qualities of leadership aren't innate to each individual, but developed over years of practice, mistake-making, and fine-tuning. Leaders gain confidence from cleaning up the many messes they make, attempting to do better the next time. And it's a constantly evolving role depending on the age, stage, and readiness level of those they lead or parent. Caring for an infant requires a different parenting style from coping with an adolescent or relating to offspring as adults. Managing a brand-new employee involves much more direction and coaching than a senior one who demands further delegation and empowerment. And a smart family business owner would never hand the reins of leadership to a next-generation family member unless they were ready and able to do the job successfully.

It's also true that not all leaders are positive exemplars of integrity and good behavior. Some can be power-hungry, malevolent, even monstrous. I've been a witness to these kinds of leaders as well, and these experiences have taught me what leadership is *not*.

Here, my focus is on the *positive* attributes of leadership. I've broken them down into eight qualities—where the behaviors, convictions, and competencies add up to

The two hardest jobs in the world: managing people at work and raising kids at home.

something more than "characteristics." I'm using the word "qualities" because I believe it better captures the whole essence of the person, not just the component parts, and fully describes how they show up to others. After I define each quality, I will provide tools and techniques to cultivate these qualities into action.

There's one more thing before we dig into the list. The leadership qualities I present add up to a power that enables these people to become transformational. Being able to inspire and to cultivate the best in others around them is the definition of true leadership, and should be the North Star for all would-be leaders.

The eight qualities are resilience, discernment, presence, collaboration, compassion, courage, knowledge of self, and knowledge of systems.

QUALITY 1

RESILIENCE

THE WORLD CONTINUES to increase in complexity and the pace of change continues to intensify, making leadership far more challenging than it has ever been.

How is it that some leaders have stamina and endurance to remain focused when others seem to struggle? What is it that allows these leaders to cope, bounce back from adversity, and even appear to thrive in the most difficult of circumstances? The answer is resilience. I've put this quality first, because without resilience, leaders can't offer any of the other qualities.

My favorite definition of this quality is "the capacity to absorb high levels of continuous change while displaying *minimal* dysfunctional behavior" (my emphasis).[4] Change is a key concept here, because many leaders imagine themselves as not simply "change managers" but also "change makers." Most leaders will profess to "embrace change" but many of them will at the same time exhibit highly dysfunctional behavior in the face of it, holding on for dear life to what was, not what could be.

Resilience isn't just what people have, it's what they *do*.

These problematic behaviors resemble our stress reactions to threat and danger. Sometimes we *freeze*, which can look like depression, helplessness, hopelessness, or feeling trapped. At other times, we *fight*, which can come across as anger, frustration, or hypervigilance in clinging to the old. And often we *flee* because we fear change or are anxious about the new and unknown. We are creatures of habit and certainty, and in our compulsion to control, we stay true to the ritual comforts of belief and behavior that provide us with the illusions of safety and order.

While some of us are fortunate enough to actually experience years of relative stability in the home and the workplace, for most of us it's really rare. The leaders who stand out are the resilient ones, flexible, adaptable, and able to navigate the vicissitudes—of varying size and degree—both planned and visited upon us all-of-a-sudden.

Resilience isn't just what people have, it's what they *do*. It's an approach to leading that supports their families and teams during adversity, be it in the midst of slight confusion, deeper chaos, or even total disruption. Resilient leaders can deftly maneuver their world into a "new normal" by responding rather than just reacting to changing conditions. They take stock of their resources, routines, and roles, and redesign their family or work systems to create order from disarray. They are optimistic.

On the resilience continuum (see below), they rank high on the nourishing end and low on the depletion end, having learned to identify and increase the conditions that give them energy, not create exhaustion. They maintain healthy personal and professional boundaries permeable enough for true understanding, but strong enough to protect themselves from others' projections, needs, and desires.

A TOOL TO CULTIVATE YOUR RESILIENCE

Most of us are moving so fast and so hard that we've lost our awareness of what gives us the energy to be healthy, well, and productive in our lives ... and what takes those things away. Here's a tool to help you identify and build your levels of resilience.

Your Resilience Continuum

The Resilience Continuum describes the conditions that deplete your energy at one end, all the way to those that expand it on the other. Expanded energy translates to supporting your mental and physical recovery from stress.

DEPLETION / EXHAUSTION Conditions that undermine my well-being and deplete me	NOURISHMENT / RECOVERY Conditions that support my well-being and nourish me
Actions driven by force	Actions driven by purpose and meaning
Removal of personal choice	Autonomy and control
Contrary to my values and ethics	Alignment with my values and ethics
Resource poor	Resource rich
Lack of support	Social engagement

Exercise: My Resilience Continuum

- Take a piece of paper and draw a vertical line down the middle. If you're on a screen, create two vertical columns.

- Informed by the conditions on the Continuum, make a list in the left column of all the situations, tasks, and relationships that drain, deplete, exhaust, and diminish you. Be as specific as possible. These conditions could include "working from home and being separated from my colleagues and their creative energy" or "being a member of the 'sandwich generation'"—responsible for the simultaneous care of your children and your parents.

- Move to the right column and list all those situations, tasks, and relationships that fill you up with energy, nourish your mind-body, and nurture your soul. Again, get very specific. These could include a "daily walk in the forest," "spending time with a dear friend," or "being in the 'flow' of a new project at work."

Then put the list in a drawer. You'll want to look at this with fresh eyes, so it is important to return to the list a few days later, adding what you hadn't thought of the first time around.

Now, to increase our resilience, we need to create as many nourishing conditions as possible, and reduce those that deplete us. It may surprise you (or comfort you!) to know that most lists are very depletion-heavy. That's okay. If it feels like a realistic start for you, that's an honest start. Your goal is to get to around 15 percent on the energy-depleting side and 85 percent on the energy-nourishing side.

The first step in bumping up the right column is to increase your awareness of where you are, what you are doing, and who you are relating to in your life. Next, you should name those nourishing and energizing elements—naming is empowering. Finally, you'll want to take action to reduce your exhaustion load by asking yourself the following questions:

- What can I remove?

- What can I transform or change?

- What can I accept with a healthy dose of self-compassion?

Examples of energy drainers are everywhere: back-to-back virtual meetings, putting up with your cousin-business-partner's idiosyncrasies, that book club you signed up for three months ago but only feel bad about.

Managing the depleting forces in your life is much easier than you think. You just need to remember: Remove, Transform, Accept. For example:

- **Remove:** Just quit the book club. Maybe next year.

- **Transform:** Create a time-blocking system to guarantee a 15-minute break between every event in your day.

- **Accept:** Learn to release that particular cousin-induced stress by practicing gratitude for the many opportunities the family business affords you and your family.

DISCERNMENT

W E ARE CONSTANTLY bombarded by information, from the trivial to the transcendent. Strong leaders need to selectively home in on what's most vital and valuable by first paying rigorous attention, and then employing good judgment to make wise decisions for each circumstance. They actively listen (one of the most valuable skills of all). And then they ask the right questions to pinpoint problems, understand needs, and identify the options. Relevance, timing, and the potential future impact on those who will be affected by their decisions all come into the mix. Finally, they must use their critical thinking skills to clearly understand each situation or problem, anticipate risks or unintended consequences, and foresee benefits. This is a long list, and it's why discernment is so critical. Knowing *how* to choose brings you and your team to the solution faster and more amicably. Not everything can be a priority.

But it's not just about employing analytical and intellectual abilities. Great leaders also have "hunches," those intuitions they investigate rather than ignore or discount. Combining both cognitive and intuitive experience, they can discern what matters most and then make a decision. Being discerning isn't the same as being decisive, but possessing this quality of constructive reflection ultimately leads to better decision-making.

A TOOL TO CULTIVATE YOUR DISCERNMENT

Leaders live in constellations of manifold circumstances that require discernment before decision-making. They need the wisdom to understand context, maintain perspective, and appreciate the interrelationships between people and systems.

Investigate Your "Sorting" Skill

This quality can be developed by an intuitive process of "sorting" through all the information being received. This skill requires intense concentration on the cues you pick up from others via their verbal, nonverbal (gestures and expressions), and paraverbal (tone or pitch) communication. Try this the next time you're in a meeting or at a family gathering:

1   Be alert to what people are saying and not saying, and how their bodies deliver messages.

2   Practice appropriate detachment and work hard to *not* insert yourself or get caught up in the story unfolding around you. This skill requires you to be externally focused on others, and to pay attention to your own internal narratives or projections.

Great leaders have intuitions they investigate rather than ignore or discount.

3   Pick up the cues by writing down all the information you are noticing. Examples:

- Your youngest son won't acknowledge your spouse. Your spouse is badgering your middle son about his homework in an aggressive tone.

- One of your direct reports is texting in the meeting and glancing at one of their colleagues after each text. The receiver returns the glance and sends a text. This keeps happening.

- The patriarch of the family business raises his voice at one grandchild, who responds with silent acquiescence.

4   Notice how your mind will naturally start sorting through the collection of cues to determine what's happening: Is the system in equilibrium or disequilibrium? How are unfolding relationships affecting each person on the team or in the family? The questions you ask will be deeper and more discerning. Your analysis of the situation will be more astute and the decisions you make will be more deliberate and attuned to the moment.

Here are examples of discerning questions—adapted from the Global Digital Citizen Foundation's Critical Thinking Skills Cheatsheet[5]—that you can ask as a way of sorting through the data before making your decisions:

- Who will be most directly affected by my decision? Who could benefit? Who could be harmed?

- What are the system's strengths and weaknesses to handle the decision—or not? Do the members have the emotional, intellectual, and relational capacity to manage the effects of the decision once it's made?

- What other perspectives or information should I seek before I decide?

- Where will this decision ultimately lead the team?

- Is there a desire or need for the family to actually deal with this situation?

- Will the decision make a real difference for the people involved?

- When is the best time to act?

PRESENCE

LEADERS SHOW UP for people. They encourage, enable, and on a good day, even inspire their followers to be their best selves. They create intentional connections, making each person feel heard and understood for the unique experience they bring to the meeting or the meal. Present leaders are steadier and have more space for curiosity. This quality allows for an openness to whatever is happening for the other person. And from that, they can have an authentic response.

As leaders, you make meaning by paying attention to the three channels of each and every message you give and receive. Always keep the "7-38-55 Rule" in mind: research reveals that only 7 percent of meaning is communicated through the words we say, 38 percent is communicated through our tone of voice, and 55 percent is revealed through our body language.[6] Leaders—when they practice presence—have an exquisite sensitivity to all three. In perceiving the myriad nuances of expression and identifying underlying feelings and hidden meanings, they are able to respond thoughtfully and articulate clearly. The rewards can be profound. A strong quality of presence deepens trust, connection, and even intimacy.

Leaders who are present acquire patience. And both presence and patience require dedicated practice. These leaders also tend to possess equanimity—a stable attitude based in mindful compassion. They can lower the volatility, volume, and temperature in the room by reconnecting to their inner calm and external level-headedness. Finally, leaders with strong presence make the most motivating mentors, coaches, parents, and partners. They're like the president of your own personal fan club!

TOOLS TO CULTIVATE YOUR PRESENCE

It's very difficult to focus on the person or on the situation in front of you when you are driven to distraction and reacting instead of responding. One of the ways to move from immediate reaction to thoughtful response is by literally learning how to pay better attention.

Tool #1: Paying Attention

1 **Commit:** Before your next family conversation or work meeting, decide to be in it. Create a distinct "conversation container": whatever you were just focused on before this encounter is set aside and you now commit to the situation you're about to enter. Send the message that you and the person in front of you are both there for exactly the same reason: to pay 100 percent attention to each other.

Before your next family conversation or work meeting, decide to be in it.

2   **Listen:** Be an active participant by responding fully through your words, tone of voice, and body language. What does that mean? Two things to start: make eye contact and give visual and/or vocal cues that you are paying attention. (Wait, there are three actually. Put away your phones. Both of them. Seriously.)

3   **Pause:** Don't be afraid of silence. Pause and reflect before jumping in to ask questions. This pause signals a respect and consideration for others' thoughts and feelings, showing that what they say really matters. Pausing will allow you to prepare a more considered and relevant response. Don't rush in before the other person has finished. True listening doesn't mean planning the next thing you are going to say while they are talking. This is a very, very hard habit to break. Pledge to start right away.

4   **Ask:** Be authentic in your questioning by staying curious. Probe into motivations and experiences. Bring those once uncomfortable questions to the surface. Build on what is being said and engage with people at a more profound level. The deeper your curiosity, the deeper the listening and the more thoughtful the responses. You are creating a continuous "growth-conversation" loop, and that will absolutely increase the investment on everyone's part. More present attention leads to more collaboration. No leader ever went wrong asking a question that began with "Tell me more about…"

Tool #2: Take Mental-Health-and-Wellness Breaks

Each day, proactively improve your ability to stay present and effective by time-blocking one 15- or 20-minute break in the morning and another in the afternoon. Putting these deliberate pauses in your schedule will increase the chances that you will actually do it, because there will always be an excuse not to. Some options for your break: eat or drink something nourishing, run up and down the stairs a few times, express gratitude for someone or something in your life, or lock yourself in a closet and just sit there quietly.

COLLABORATION

LEADING ISN'T FOR the faint of heart. It really *is* lonely at the top, and the best leaders choose collaborators, confidants, and partners from whom to seek support and with whom they can wrestle with challenges and gain perspective. No one knows the solutions to all the inherent problems that come with this gig, so the humility to ask for help, advice, feedback, and even tough love is essential.

This is important. When leaders get caught in the echo chamber of their own interior monologues, they are more susceptible to fooling themselves into thinking they are "right." This leads to making mistakes—sometimes grave and irreversible. Good leaders can flex between being in charge and being receptive. They create more win–win interactions by inviting others' contributions in exploring ideas and negotiating problems in ways that are more nuanced, expansive, and respectful of their followers.

Finally, collaboration is an effective way to manage the many stresses of leadership because it acts as a form of co-regulation. Research shows that deepening our connections with others in an environment of safety can actually calm our nervous systems and settle our bodies.[7] Connecting keeps us curious, more reasonable, and open to possibilities. In any crisis—and, for most leaders, crises are commonplace—people become anxious, which makes them more "threat-rigid" and risk-averse. Here, they invariably revert back to what worked in the past. But, if leaders are *collaborative* during a crisis, the chances for successful resolution improve. It also works to enhance the success of the whole system coming together: colleagues feel more invested in the outcomes and in each other.

TOOLS TO CULTIVATE YOUR COLLABORATION

Creating partnerships with trusted colleagues, learning how to count on others for advice, and sharing vulnerabilities are all obvious skills for leaders to develop. But collaboration can be tough. It's difficult to cede power and control (even the benevolent kind) when you believe that the final accountability for the health and success of your family and your organization rests with *you*. For collaboration to work, there needs to be deep trust between you and your collaborators, and a sense of psychological safety to let you lower your guard (and ego). The art of engaging the collective intelligence of your work team and family members will help you reach the best result or decision.

In business, when department leaders take on a lone-wolf approach—digging in their heels and alienating their colleagues who lead other teams—they create departmental silos, which often leads to dysfunction across the entire system. See if this sounds familiar: M, a new VP of marketing, unilaterally decides to redefine how the company will advertise their products, and restructures the marketing department accordingly to support this strategy. These changes affect the long-established workflow patterns and relationships between M's department and those of customer service and procurement. Relations between all the leaders and their respective teams are increasingly strained. The new strategies clash with the old processes. Each department becomes more entrenched in their opposing positions, and the entire company culture is negatively affected. Here, if M had collaborated with her colleagues from the start—across departments, not just in marketing—together they might have smashed the silos instead of deepening them.

In family-enterprise systems, fiefdoms are created when leaders are unable to collaborate. I have seen how a dominant and controlling owner created an insular family business, perceiving all the rising generation's new ideas as threats to his fragile ego. J led through fear, and created a culture of "yes" people who were unable to assert their own agency. They actually referred to J as "The King" and to themselves as his "minions." For years they felt too insecure and anxious to leave the company... until they found the courage to strike out on their own.

Tool #1: Create (and Expand) Your Trusted Network Circle

Actually, create two networks—one for home and one for work. Draw a circle (that's you) and then draw two concentric circles around you. In the first ring, write the names of

For collaboration to work, **there needs to be deep trust** between you and your collaborators.

people you trust: your most trusted current collaborators, mentors, advice-givers, and compassionate constructive critics. In the second ring, write down names of who you'd be interested in building relationships with for their experience/reputation/interests. Connect with everyone in those rings, using whatever communication vehicle they prefer. Extend appreciation to your first-tier collaborators for being in your circle. Send your potential collaborators an invitation to connect in a safe and casual way. Whoever responds to your request is a first sign of who you will want to recruit into your circle.

Tool #2: Foster Your Own Collaborative Style

I have used a collaboration framework developed by one of my brilliant mentors, Lorne Plunkett, and his colleague Robert Fournier, for over twenty years—and always to great effect. I am so grateful to them for this model they call "Participative Management."[8] In essence, there are three decision-making approaches that leaders can use to increase the commitment of their employees over time.

Independent decision-making: It's your decision, everyone knows it, and you have all the information you need to make it.

Collaborative decision-making: It's your decision, everyone knows it, and you are open to receiving the input of others' perspectives, feelings, and opinions to help inform your decision so it can be the best for the situation.

Empowered decision-making: You willingly relinquish your power to an individual or a group who is ready and able to make the decision, but you don't disappear. You offer clear guidelines, and can be a coach if they need your support.

Parents can apply these same styles as they gradually seek the input and participation of the kids in family decision-making.

Here's an exercise to increase your awareness of the decision-making styles you use as a leader at home and at work.

1   What are the **independent** decisions you make as a leader? Here are some helpful reminders as you analyze each decision:

- There is always a role for decisive leadership.

- Not all decisions should be shared.

- These kinds of decisions are made so you can get on with other activities and not be victim to "paralysis by analysis."

- Independent decisions are often easily accepted and expected by your team and family members.

And here's a helpful phrase to clarify that this is your decision to make: "I need to gather some information before I make a decision."

2   What **collaborative** decisions do you make? Here are some guidelines:

- This is the first level of sharing a decision, so the key factor is your willingness to be *influenced* by your team and family members.

- This is the most common and most *misunderstood* leadership style. People think that when a leader asks them for their thoughts, feelings, biases, and ideas, this makes the decision a mutual one. A common refrain I hear is this: "Well, if she asked me for my opinion, then why didn't she take it?" In this style, the leader asks for others' input, but still retains the right to make the decision.

- Think of this style not as group decision-making, rather as leader decision-making with the strongly welcomed influence of an individual or a group.

- Communication is critical. Share your decision once you've made it and explain your rationale when possible.

Here's a helpful phrase: "Thanks for your help. I'll let you know what I decide." Notice the "I" as a reminder of who's ultimately making the decision.

3   Which of your decisions are based on *empowerment*, where you place the responsibility in the hands of an individual team or family member or the entire group?

-   Don't confuse this style with abdication. You're still able to be involved as a facilitator or coach or even an equal participant in the decision-making process.

-   This is the very best strategy to lead when the highest level of commitment is required to achieve the best implementation of a decision or a project.

-   Your job is to offer clear and specific guidelines to ensure the decision-makers' success. For example: deadlines for decisions to be made, the financial resources available for the project they are deciding on, and confirmation that the decision must be in accordance with the organization's and/or family's values.

COMPASSION

COMPASSION IS EMPATHY in action. Michael Ventura, author of *Applied Empathy: The New Language of Leadership,* writes, "Getting out of your own perspective and seeing the world through different eyes will help you be a better leader."[9] Empathy is also feeling *with* someone—it's the resonance of emotion that beats in the spaces between. Neuroscientific research shows that compassion takes empathy one positive step further. Since empathic responses can actually generate the pain centers in a person's central nervous system, that leaves both parties in a state of suffering.[10] Compassion is different because it opens the pleasure (dopamine) centers in our brain by first connecting to that suffering, and then manifesting it as an action. This action reduces the discomfort for everyone.

Just by asking the simple question "How can I help?" leaders offer a message of active engagement, generosity of spirit, and purposeful connection.

Compassion is empathy in action.

TOOLS TO CULTIVATE YOUR COMPASSION

Cultivating compassion is paying attention to other people, and then helping them reduce whatever distress they may be experiencing. But leaders often forget to care for and appreciate *themselves,* because serving the needs of others always seems to take precedence. Like putting on your own oxygen mask first on an airplane, it's helpful to offer generous attention to yourself before you give it to everyone else. Think of it as giving the gift of self-compassion.

Tool #1: Develop Compassion and Appreciation for Yourself

1   At the end of your day, reflect on what you've done *well.* Name the actions you took and the words you said that were smart, helpful, and had a positive impact on you, your family, and your workplace, such as asking yourself, "What did I do to ... "

- foster my relationships?
- grow my business?
- manage my time effectively?
- improve my skills and behaviors?

Everyone's tendency is to pay attention to the negative and identify all the things that went wrong, what they could've done better, and how badly they feel. This psychological phenomenon is called "negativity bias." It is our tendency to not only register and react more readily to negative stimuli than positive experiences, but also to dwell on these events more deeply and more often.[11] From an evolutionary perspective, paying attention to negative threats ensured survival. Recent neurological research shows that our brains have a much stronger response to negative thoughts and images than to positive ones.[12] So the effects of this bias can be harmful and limiting to our self-perception, our relationships, and our decision-making.[13] That's why a deliberate practice of noticing and taking in the positive (self-compassion) is so critical. Focusing your attention on the positive aspects of your deeds and words will increase your psychological health, happiness, and even success.

2 There are many compassion or loving-kindness practices you can invite into your daily life. You can come up with your own phrases to generously wish yourself well by repeating them silently in your mind as many times as you wish. Here are a few of my favorites:

May I be safe, be happy, be healthy, and live with ease. [14]

May I be filled with loving kindness.
May I be peaceful and at ease.
May I be healthy and well.
May I be happy.

Tool #2: Develop Compassion and Appreciation for Others

Approach a family member, a colleague, or a team member who is wrestling with a specific problem or having a difficult time overall and ask, "What can I do?" Remember, you don't need to know the answer. Simply by asking the question, you are transforming the empathy *you* feel into a compassionate action to help reduce *their* discomfort. The answer might be as simple as offering your undivided attention to brainstorm solutions, or as complicated as supporting them to make a plan for a radical life change. Offering compassionate action increases the interconnectedness between you and others, strengthens relationships, and creates a reciprocal circle of giving and receiving. Everyone benefits.

COURAGE

LEADERS NEED A special kind of grit in order to grind through the daily tests of their role. Constantly pushed out of their comfort zones, effective leaders are determined to keep going when anxious and afraid. Leadership is a never-ending balance between controlling distractions and maximizing focus—all the while attending to the demands of the people to whom they are accountable. With these competing responsibilities, conflict is inevitable. And conflict is where we begin our discussion of courage.

Most of us are experts at avoiding conflict, but leaders can't elude or deny it. Conflict comes in many flavors: the differences of opinion at home or at work, the tensions of a quiet skirmish or the battles of an outright war, the hurt feelings from a miscommunication, an organizational power struggle, or a pernicious family narrative. Pretending that the conflict doesn't exist won't make it disappear, and the longer it stays hidden, the worse the problems— and often more damaged the relationships—become. Conflict often shows up as resentment, passive-aggressive behavior, or emotional withdrawal.

Leaders have to make difficult decisions that can disappoint, anger, and destabilize. They have to say "no" while being very aware that they may have to pay a hefty price for setting limits. When making the wrong call, they need to willingly and humbly admit their mistakes, and forgive themselves for not always having the answer. (There will, inevitably, be many more chances to learn from those mistakes.) And they ought to forgo their need for unwavering love, approval, and admiration. All of these actions require tremendous courage.

Every time I've asked an organizational leader later in their career to share a regret, the response is, without exception, their lack of courage to deal effectively with conflict. This usually takes the form of retaining employees who should have been terminated. For partners, it's not attending to the conflicts in the relationship early enough to prevent their decline into deep misery. And for parents, it's their inability to say "no" to their kids when they should have because they just wanted to avoid rejection or (another) explosion. It's a tall order to reject complacency and cultivate courage. But leaders have to be comfortable *enough* in the discomfort of conflict to dive in and work to find resolution.

A TOOL TO CULTIVATE YOUR COURAGE

We have all been bewildered, fraught with worry, and even roiled with resentment over a conflict that seemed unresolvable. Conflict can destroy relationships, derail progress, and create antipathy among team and family members—even if they're not directly involved in the specific conflict. Most of the time, these conflicts are "disappeared"—pushed down never to be discussed—because the risks in addressing them are considered too high. This leaves the parties stuck in that dance of discomfort, pretending that it's all fine but knowing it's really not. Leading with courage means dealing with the dread and taking on the conflict.

The 3 Cs of a Courageous Conversation

If you're in a conflict with someone, then they're in a conflict with you (even if they claim ignorance). Be the first to name it out loud. Then introduce these preparatory tools to your counterpart to let them know you're doing everything possible to reflect on and prepare for a constructive and ultimately positive conversation with them about it. Invite them to do the same. This will send them a message that the relationship matters to you. The conversation will be a catalyst for both of you to develop curiosity, concern, and care for each other.

Curiosity

- What *really* happened that led to this conflict?

- Which mental models—the assumptions and stories that you carry about yourselves, your family, other people, organizations, and every aspect of the world—shaped your experience of and conclusions about the situation?

- How can you analyze the situation with a curiosity lens to challenge your mental models?

Leading with courage means dealing with the dread and taking on the conflict.

Concern

- What do you think is the true issue for your counter-part? (Examples could include their ability to be part of the team, the effect of their decisions on the whole system, their mental health, or their future employability.)

- How can you express your concern to them so they can hear and believe you without reacting defensively?

Care

- In this courageous conversation, what is your *most desired outcome* for...

  1 yourself?
  2 your counterpart?
  3 your relationship?
  4 your work team, your family, your family business?

- To communicate your desired outcomes compassionately, what can you say and how can you say it through your body language and tone of voice?

KNOWLEDGE OF SELF

INTELLIGENCE COMES IN many forms. The differentiator that sets true leaders apart is their emotional and social intelligence. Leaders have self-knowledge (a heightened awareness and understanding of one's own signature of emotions and consequent behaviors), and the ability to appropriately manage it through self-control and discernment (knowing when to keep your inside voice from being shared outside).

Daniel Goleman disrupted the world of leadership theory with the publication of his best-selling book *Emotional Intelligence: Why It Can Matter More Than IQ* (1995), when he introduced the idea that leadership is about *more* than the person's intellectual superiority. Leaders with a high emotional intelligence quotient (EIQ), he argues, can name their internal states of mind and heart, manage their own disruptive emotions, and maintain a positive mindset and an adaptable attitude.

Leaders are always part of a system and **must be expert at maneuvering** through its different constellations.

ASK FOR FEEDBACK

Your assessment of how you show up at home and at work won't always align with how your team and your family experience you. That's because you aren't aware of your own blind spots. Common leadership blind spots I have witnessed (more than a few times) include the leaders being so focused on getting through their meeting agenda that they don't notice that everyone but them is on their phone and no one is fully present, withholding emotional support or recognition of a job well done for fear of giving someone a swelled head, and being so in love with their own ideas that they only pretend to consider others' input, having already made up their minds.

The best tool to gauge your levels of self-awareness and self-management is by asking for honest feedback. But it doesn't need to be a formal, complicated, multi-question, 360-degree online assessment (which makes everyone very nervous, by the way). This can simply be a tool for constructive reflection about your behaviors, and it can consist of a few very simple questions to fit your unique leadership context:

- How am I being effective in supporting/challenging/loving/attending to you? Can you please give me some specific examples of what and how I'm showing that?

- What else could I start saying or doing to offer you more support/challenge/love/attention?

- What would you like me to stop doing? Please be specific.

Here's a bonus to implementing this tool: when you model true openness to receiving feedback, it will make it easier for your family and team members to ask for and accept feedback themselves.

Deepening one's self-awareness and emotional self-management is essential for leaders. But these qualities are not enough on their own. Because leaders are always part of a system, they must be expert at maneuvering through its different constellations and the relationships within them.

KNOWLEDGE OF SYSTEMS

A S I DESCRIBED in the introduction, each domain
we inhabit is a system made up of people and the
relationships that connect them. Effective leaders
are systems thinkers, possessing a holistic understanding
and knowledge of how the separate, constituent parts of a
system interrelate within the context of its environment.
My wise teacher and generous mentor, Jay Lappin, writes:

> Families are living, open and dynamic systems com-
> posed of individuals who are connected in special ways
> that mutually affect one another. They have patterns of
> relating that are interdependent, complementary and
> necessary for carrying out their lives, and they have
> rules and structures to survive, live and thrive.[15]

Workplaces are systems too, influenced by people, events,
and circumstances both inside and outside their walls
(standing or virtual), where every department, team, and

employee is interconnected in order to best serve the company's stakeholders and achieve its goals. Leaders at home and at work see these contextual connections, and are guided by the understanding that the whole is greater than the sum of its parts.

It follows, then, that great leaders also possess a sharp social awareness. Expert at "reading the room," they are highly sensitive to others and savvy about the dynamics of the different systems in which they are participating. Because they can pick up on different personality styles, emotional cues, and communication signals, they are able to manage their relationships effectively, influence broadly, and inspire easily.

A TOOL TO CULTIVATE YOUR SYSTEMS KNOWLEDGE

Design a Social Systems Mind Map

Choose a situation at home or at work that requires an action or decision from you. This situation might be an opportunity, challenge, or change. Draw a map of all the people that affect or will be affected in that system by the position you take, and how. Considering the context is so critical to an effective response. It's rarely a linear process, and will force you to think laterally and recognize all the people—the individual pieces of the puzzle—who contribute to the whole situation.

Here are a couple of quick stories to illustrate how the map can be helpful.

Great leaders are expert at "reading the room."

One of my therapy clients, CJ, had been considering divorce for many years, but felt stuck because of all the people whose "lives would be ruined." We sat down and together drew a map of her social system. I asked CJ to describe how her divorce would affect each person ... in detail. The exercise helped her realize that she was projecting her own fears, biases, and judgments onto them. She had lost a sense of proportion about the scope of her action, and apart from CJ's grown children who would be sad and concerned for their parents' future happiness and financial security, their lives and those of the other people on the map would not be "destroyed."

L, a family business founder and owner, employed his two children and one nephew. He was considering whom to choose as his successor. Based on work performance, skills, and attitude, his youngest child was the best candidate. But it wasn't a simple or straightforward business decision. L needed to account for all the possible consequences that the choice would have in the overlapping family relationships—between spouses, children, grandchildren, siblings, and cousins. He prepared a family map with each person's name written in a separate circle. Then I gave him different lines to draw (double, solid, broken, very faint, and so on) between the circles—the connections—which would indicate how the relationships would look if he chose his youngest child. The visual representation was a powerful gauge of the damage and dysfunction this would cause in the family dynamics, and confirmed L's worries.

So he changed course. We introduced a fair and transparent practice to determine a successor and reduce the chance of future family disharmony. The five elements of a fair process we adhered to were as follows:

1   Communication: giving a voice to all members.

2   Clarity: setting clear expectations of what competencies were required for succession.

3   Consistency: committing to the process and treating all members the same.

4   Changeability: believing that change is possible for all and that what was true before is not necessarily true now.

5   Commitment to fairness: being able to work on the process together and questioning ourselves as we move through it.[16]

PART TWO

WHAT TO DO AS A LEADER

The 8 Lessons

NOW THAT YOU are familiar with the qualities of leadership, it's time to move to the lessons of leadership.

Great leaders are—without exception—ambitious, goal-oriented, and results-driven. What they do to inspire others to thrive—personally and professionally, day in and day out—is complex and demanding. But it's also rewarding and impactful. I believe that leading any kind of social system (family or business) is the hardest job in the world. (Seriously, I tell my clients that they "deserve a medal for just getting out of bed every morning!") Presidents, partners, and parents do this heroic work because they are driven to—not for the glory, but to make a discernible difference to the everyday experiences of their families and their teams.

To describe what effective leaders do, I've identified a number of recurring themes that have guided my diverse and successful clients over the decades. I've organized these themes into eight lessons, forming a leadership

Presidents, partners, and parents do this heroic work to make a discernible difference.

roadmap you can use to foster and preserve nourishing, productive, and whole systems at home and at work.

I will describe each lesson through case studies gathered from the three domains of family, business, and family enterprise, and I'll identify the crossovers between them. At the end of each lesson, I'll offer *you* some "homework" to support your reflections and actions on the leadership theme presented.

Here are the 8 essential leadership lessons:

1 **Values:** Know what you believe in.
2 **Mission:** Determine your purpose.
3 **Vision:** Aspire toward a compelling future.
4 **Strategy:** Make a plan and set the goals to achieve it.
5 **Governance:** Create a safe container.
6 **Change:** Manage uncertainty without losing your center.
7 **Relationships:** Nurture and inspire the best in everyone.
8 **Legacy:** Foster continuity and a well-planned succession.

VALUES

Know What You Believe In

IF YOU DON'T STICK
TO YOUR VALUES WHEN
THEY'RE BEING TESTED,
THEY'RE NOT VALUES:
THEY'RE HOBBIES.

JON STEWART

GUIDE. MANIFESTO. COMPASS. Philosophy. These are just some of the ways that people describe a set of intrinsic values or beliefs. I think of them as a kind of *cultural connective tissue* that holds the structure and members together in both work and family systems.

I know that "cultural connective tissue" sounds like an intangible construct, but when I ask people to define their culture, they usually default to the actions that happen in their workplace: "It's just how we do things around here," or "We have a culture of always checking with management before we make a move like that," or "Working overtime here is expected; it shows commitment to the brand." But in reality, these remarks belie distinct contours of their corporate culture. They may as well say, "This company is stuck in inertia, and there doesn't seem to be a desire to change," and "This is a culture of micromanagement," and "This company overworks its employees and burns them out. And they keep doing it."

And even the move from *actions* to *culture* still doesn't present a holistic picture. What we're really talking about here are values.

It's critical to know what you stand for, even if it may feel impossible to describe. Naming what matters most opens the door to mutual understanding, meaningful communication, and authentic connection. It strengthens the bonds and clarifies what's okay and what's not in how you treat each other. It's your mission's operating manual. Moving from the amorphous to the discernible, you can discover home and work values and the specific behaviors that embody them.

The discovery of your core values isn't a shopping expedition. You can't pick and choose what may look nice or sound good or impress. It's a journey into uncovering the cultural soul of your family or your company. Digging deep to figure out what really matters—what are the dealbreakers, the guiding principles, the lines in the sand—will set the glue that holds the system together over time.

But time and circumstances are different. Values don't alter with a change of context, and ultimately, they are what consistently guide your decisions and keep you sane. When life's challenges arise—and especially when a crisis hits—your values define what you know to be true. And this knowledge will help to get you through.

VALUES CASE STUDY: HOME

This case focuses on a recently blended family, who needed to create a unified and distinct set of values in order to articulate what mattered most for all its members.

D, one of the spouses, had two daughters with her husband of 15 years and truly believed she was living a full, contented life. And then, all of a sudden, when the girls were 10 and 12, D fell head over heels for K, a single mother who had a son at the same middle school. Their relationship exploded into furtive and secret meetings for six months until they got themselves "caught."

This falling-in-love business can turn perfectly reasonable people into risk-takers and troublemakers. Here, they got sloppy and left too many texts and emails undeleted, leading to their exposure. Chaos ensued. The girls' father, O, first retreated in denial and then, in anger, tried to sue for full custody. Because they wanted O to be present in his children's lives, D and K asked him to enter a formal mediation process so that the best interests of the children could be front and center. Ultimately he agreed, which allowed the drama between the adults to eventually die down.

But when the new couple and their kids moved in together, there was more upheaval. How could two distinct family systems become a functional blended one? A pathway to acceptance of their "new normal" was to figure out what this different family configuration could believe in and how they would treat each other with compassion. They needed to figure out their shared values.

That's when I was invited into their home life. The first series of conversations started with the adults. D and K needed to more fully understand all the complexities and challenges of blended family life, and how to cope with this massive transition. Then the two women had to find a unified and coherent voice, offering the same messages to the kids. We'll revisit the notion of a shared voice in a later lesson, but here are just some of the issues they had to address before they could get there.

Transitioning into a blended family requires a lot of time and effort for everyone to adjust to all the change, and it can take several years to find a place of ease and relative comfort for all its members. Immediately upon forming this new family system, there are "insiders" and "outsiders." For example, the parent–child bond can leave the other adult feeling like a powerless outsider, lonely, and even rejected. This is especially true when moms or dads have been single-parenting for a while and now there's another adult in the picture. The kids can feel like they matter less to their stepparent, giving way to jealousies, insecurities, and resentments.

Conflicting loyalties are very common in these family systems. Often children worry and wonder whether, if they care about—or even start to love—the stepparent, it means that they are being disloyal to the "real" parent. And oh, the unrealistic expectations on the parents' part! In these situations, they are so freaked out about being the perfect stepparent that I have to lower the bar. I tell them to "just let go of your need to be loved by your stepchildren any-time soon. Be satisfied with civility and respect from them. If love arrives over time, that's a wonderful gift, but it is absolutely not guaranteed, nor can it be expected."

Beyond the stepparent, there was another "outsider" in this family to consider, and that was O, the girls' dad (the father of K's son was no longer in the picture). In order to decrease conflict, mixed messages and confusion, all the parents must learn to work out their issues away from the kids, creating an impenetrable boundary between the generations. Triangulation is always a bad practice in families of separation and divorce. This is a term we use to describe "a relational pattern where two family members entangle a third individual into their relationship"[17] to balance excessive intimacy, conflict, or distance, and to provide stability in the system. In this situation the relationship between the mom and the dad was triangulated because O was using the kids to communicate with D, instead of dealing with her directly.

Adults need courage to practice healthy and clear communication (maybe for the first time) so the kids don't get caught in the crossfire. Almost always, children don't have an easy time understanding and accepting *why* their parents split up. Introducing a new partner into the family home and asking them to adjust to that person and *their* children can exacerbate their sense of confusion, loss, and fear.

Everyone wants to feel loved and supported. Research shows that developing strong social connections can actually regulate the calming and restoring parts of our nervous systems. A specific part of our parasympathetic nervous system, called the "ventral vagal nerve network," becomes activated when we connect with another person, and this triggers calmness.[18] Engaging with others helps us feel safe and sound, and we hope that families are the social systems that provide that safety.

One way that blended families can build those supportive bonds is to create new and unique ways to function. And what lies underneath these new dynamics—what makes them meaningful, resonant, and sustainable—is a set of shared values.

Let's take a look at how this worked with our family in transition...

When coming together and establishing shared values, I find it very useful to start with the parents. Here I asked D and K three questions:

1   What do you want your family to look like?

2   How do you want to be treated by everyone?

3   What will help you feel safe and happy at home?

Let's unpack those questions a bit, and shine a light on why I start with the parents. The first question (What do you want your family to look like?) seems pretty vague, and it's intentionally so. I want the family to supply their own adjectives, their own characteristics, their own "features" in the answer. The second question (How do you want to be treated by everyone?) makes things clearer, since it gets at the very personal, and demands a subjective response. The third question (What will help you feel safe and happy at home?) is actually the most powerful of all, since it invites a response that starts with care.

When I repeat these questions with the children, they have a couple of options—they can "agree" with what D and K said, in essence mirroring their thoughts and feelings, or they can very much depart from what their parents said, contributing their own needs and desires into the mix, and creating agency with their own voices. Either way, progress is made... just by having these conversations.

The discovery of your **core values** isn't a shopping expedition.

It was uncomfortable and turbulent for the first year, and required a tremendous amount of compassion and presence from the grownups. Of course it did... three adolescents in one room bringing all the complexities of that age and stage, plus the emotional toll of stepfamily development! Then something shifted, and they began to identify enough similarities between the five of them to construct a new language for the family they were all building together. We called them Fresh Start Values.

VALUES: THE CROSSOVER

In this case study, the "leaders" at home made a thoughtful and deliberate decision to take action in order to avoid further turmoil and uncertainty. Defining their values helped D and K bounce back from the kids' resistance and reconnect to their inner resilience as a couple in order to get their family through the transition from two distinct family systems to a well-functioning blended one.

But that's not always the story. In many organizational settings, the leaders do not explicitly define their values and end up with a workplace culture that is fuzzy. "Fuzzy" isn't exactly a clinical term, but it's a way of describing those well-meaning motherhood statements that just say nothing to explain what they expect from their staff. Common motherhood statements are "We live with integrity," or "We treat everyone with respect," or "We communicate effectively." This lack of specificity often leads to confusion and problem behavior. It is a sign that they too might need to refresh their values at work, just like the blended family did at home.

VALUES CASE STUDY: WORK

I am often called into a meeting by a leader who's dealing with an issue that requires an outside eye, an unbiased perspective, an "expert" to fix whatever is going wrong. Invariably, the identified problem is a person, and the symptoms are always that person's long-term behaviors. Accordingly, I ask the leader: "What are your organization's values?" And responding like a discomfited deer in the headlights, they give the standard list: integrity, pride, commitment, and so on. I ask, "How do those values translate into specific and observable behaviors by the people in your organization?" And then the leader says: "Huh? I don't understand what you mean."

This happens more than it doesn't. When the values and the behaviors reflecting those values are not clearly defined, accepted, and inculcated into a company's everyday culture, people behave badly. And it's really not their fault. Those "problem" employees are usually well-intentioned and committed employees who are either confused or are not being held accountable by their organization's leadership.

The following case study illustrates how ambiguous organizational values can make people feel disengaged, irritable, and even irrational.

S, a senior director, consistently challenged her colleagues when a major company decision was being wrangled. She sincerely believed that her candor in communicating her concerns and criticisms (loudly and proudly) added a necessary counterpoint to the conversations. Yet the team perceived S as a doomsayer—obstinate, arrogant, negative, and stubborn. The CEO wanted her gone. But honesty and communication were the company's firmly held values—at least it said so on the website and the posters in the lunchroom. Wasn't S just behaving in accordance with those values?

This senior management team needed a formal "values reset." Here's an exercise we did to discover what mattered most to them as leaders of this firm. Essentially, we created a *Values Inventory* based on the actual, lived experience of the participants—not on the idealized, Googled version of what corporate values should be.

Each member of the leadership team took a turn being the *Storyteller*. I invited them to answer this question: When did you feel most committed and proud to be a leader of this company? And I helped them build a story around that moment with the following prompts:

- Describe the situation.

- Describe your role in it.

- Describe the actions you took.

- Describe what made you so proud, and more committed than ever to your work and the company.

All the other leaders were the *Story Keepers*. I asked them to listen *very* carefully for the values or behaviors that could be identified from their colleague's story... things like "honesty" or "teamwork" or "equality." At the end of each story, we went around the room and the Story Keepers shared the specific values that they heard.

Through this collaborative process, we co-created an inventory of what mattered to each Storyteller, and were then able to identify and clarify the values they shared as company executives. And there were three: creativity, courage, and loving their customers.

The next step was bridging the divide between "what you believe" and "what you do." In essence, it's a matter of how your actions reveal your values, but here, we are inverting the order: If a company values "honesty and integrity," for example, exactly how do the actions of its employees manifest those values? What do they actually *do*?

I divided the team into three groups, assigned each a value, and asked them to describe the specific behaviors to which they would hold themselves, each other, and all their employees accountable. For example: Courage translated into "We do not avoid conflict. When there are differences of opinion, tension, or lack of clarity in our team, we deal with them in an open, curious, and compassionate way." Loving our customers was defined as "We listen to our customers. We respond to their requests within 24 hours max. We keep every promise we make. We ask them for feedback after every service." These values became the foundation upon which they made business decisions, managed differences, and achieved corporate goals. As for S, the CEO did not fire her. Instead, he invited her to actively participate in this exercise. Once the values were co-created by and explicitly stated within the executive team, she behaved in accordance with them. She, like everyone else, just needed clarity.

For family-run businesses, there are many tools out there to help identify their shared values. One favorite is *The Values Edge Kit*, developed by Dennis Jaffe and Cynthia Scott. Their model is based on 7 value categories that help people identify their personal motivations and life choices. Another effective tool is the set of *Motivational Values Cards,* produced by the philanthropic consultancy 21/64, which help affluent families identify those values that most motivate their personal, financial, and giving decisions. When I work with business families (especially those in periods of conflict and concern), these tools have proven to be the most effective (and least threatening). They help to break down communication barriers and create a safe and enjoyable environment to share personal values. They also make the process nonjudgmental and allow for an appreciation of differences, since not everything that matters to one member matters to another. Once each member articulates their individual values, we collaborate to identify what values they hold in common (and there always are some!). From there, they are on their way to creating a statement of their unique family values.

There are many benefits to facilitating these kinds of conversations. Indeed, research shows several that strongly motivate family-enterprise clients:[19]

- They form the foundation for family culture and create a shared vocabulary.

- They provide a template for collaborative decision-making.

- They inspire and motivate family members to believe in what they're doing.

- They create the system's resilience to support a patient, long-term view, which encourages members to further strengthen their family and assure a shared legacy.

- They elevate the discussion to a higher level—about family pride, responsibility, purpose, and meaning.

There is power in a group of people agreeing on a set of values and the behaviors that define those values. This can create meaningful connections and deepen our experience of belonging. It's a psychological need to be part of a family, a work team, or a family business, and it is the foundation that most of us need in order to safely develop self-esteem and a sense of accomplishment. Knowing what matters and sharing those values with our colleagues and loved ones can make a difference in how we lead with compassion.

HOME
WORK

Answer this question: What are the values that you believe in?

Find a colleague who is a leader and do the storyteller/ story keeper exercise with them. Remember that you are describing a situation, your role in it, and the actions you took that made you proud and more committed than ever to your work and the company.

Take turns.

Use these prompts to help you:

- What would people say about you as a leader?

- What are you most proud of doing?

- Who are you most proud of being?

MISSION

Determine
Your Purpose

MY MISSION IN LIFE IS NOT
MERELY TO SURVIVE, BUT
TO THRIVE; AND TO DO SO
WITH SOME PASSION, SOME
COMPASSION, SOME HUMOR,
AND SOME STYLE.

MAYA ANGELOU

BELIEVE THAT PURPOSE is the organizing principle of human systems—it's like a steady heartbeat that pumps deep meaning into its members' cells. Or think about it like DNA, the template of each system that creates a lasting language or a code of existence.

So many of us are on autopilot as we move though each day, not necessarily without aim but often without passion and focus. It's amazing to see how enlivened we can become when we do the work to define or reconnect with our purpose. Determining our purpose creates a sense of psychic stability, security, and presence, helping us cope with life's ambiguities and anxieties. It lifts us out of the dank, dark craters of self-indulgence and obsessive self-interest, and brings us into the light of authentic connection with the external world. Defining a shared creation of a family or organizational mission can fulfill our need to belong, and let's face it, for most of us, that on its own can calm our nervous systems down. It allows us to consider what we do, why we do it, and for whom. A mission clarifies the opportunity to make an impact on and contribution to our families, our workplaces, and our communities.

When we are aligned with our mission, we are powerful. We can be the active drivers, rather than the passive followers, of our fates. But when we don't have purpose, we feel lost and powerless. We move into confusion and even suffering. We get overwhelmed, flooded with information or emotion, and can only respond by contracting into our pain and bewilderment. We tend to invest less and less in our relationships, both at home and at work—even if it's only in one of those domains where our purpose is lacking. Once this investment wanes, two things typically follow: disengagement and alienation.

MISSION CASE STUDY: HOME

This story of marital breakdown shows how a couple's years of reactivity to each other's behavior led to the erosion of their purpose and of the parental leadership required to keep the family system stable and strong.

She lives in rage, he in fear, and they share equally the resentment room. C and V have been building a house of disappointment for almost two decades, all the while trying to raise a daughter with complete focus and devotion. It is an admirable feat. Despite their relationship trouble, they are such steadfast parents, openly recognizing each other's gifts in the partnership of child-raising. Nevertheless, the atmosphere is one of intermittent, quiet warfare. The wrong word, a sidelong glance, an exasperated gesture, a tone of voice can trigger each into sudden and frozen

When we are aligned with our mission, we can be the **active drivers of our fates.**

silence. It's shutdown and then lockdown, a seesaw of feeling misunderstood and overlooked, a miasma of discord and recrimination. All this in front of a very sensitive teenager who picks up on every dysfunctional cue, and has for years.

C and V are unable to connect to the whole purpose of their marriage. They are surprised by this, because the story they tell is that their union was a thoughtful and mutually desired act of joining together with God, family, and friends bearing witness. That authentic quality of the original intention is utterly lost ... or perhaps hiding?

And here I am in the middle of their battle, breathing in and breathing out, holding the container of relative safety. Trying to ensure that knives are not drawn so the blood is not visibly running onto the white leather sofa where they sit. They won't meet each other's gaze because that means connection, compassion, and intimacy—qualities that are absent for now. Instead, C and V look at me ... for translation, for advocacy, for saving them with morsels of hope. I am their point of contact but I cannot bleed with them. I can, though, invite them to move toward each other, stay where they are, or move further apart.

These are the stances of every relationship:

- Come closer.
- Stay where you are.
- Go away.[20]

Let's delve into these a bit, since they are so clear and obvious on the face of it, yet often opaque to the spouses until pointed out.

Come closer. This is the highest form of intimacy. It is to divulge one's inner landscape to another, not just in the limerence phase (that state of infatuation or obsession with another), but later and throughout, when the sheen has worn off and the years of togetherness have unraveled the initial enchantment... when the dirt starts to show. This is the stance of curiosity. When partners take the time to have those uninterrupted conversations and meaningful connections, they leave the surface communication and can plunge into the depths of discovering each other's desires, fears, strengths, and vulnerabilities. A common example is talking about sex, especially when it's bad sex or no sex. When couples are able to have those conversations, their emotional bond deepens and their sexual connection can follow.

Stay where you are. This stance can sometimes signal ambivalence, but it's also a state of apathy, paralysis, exhaustion, or boredom. I ask couples which of these barriers prevents them from inviting intimacy back into their partnership. Is it fear of being hurt or shamed? Did something happen to decrease their interest? Where did the energy they once had for the relationship go?

Go Away. You would think that this would be the clearest signal that the door to intimacy is permanently closed. But not always. Confronting a partner can be so overwhelming that pushing them away feels like the only possible response. The "negative benefit" of shutting down intimacy in relationships is self-protection. But I ask partners, "Would your stance be so definitive if you had the tools to share your vulnerabilities?"

I have learned that every marriage is really a novel-in-conversation. It can take the form of an ongoing melodrama, a short tragicomedy, a sustaining success of friendly comforts with a crisis punctuating now and then to keep it interesting. It can be a slog, a bore, a pleasure, a passion. And from what I've witnessed, most relationships inhabit all those states in an ever-shifting landscape over the course of its life.

C and V were stuck in a very negative conversation. Despite their valiant attempts to keep it together for their teenager, the rancor, confusion, and constriction in the marriage was the air that everyone breathed.

So how can they reconnect to the purpose that brought them together in the first place? The first step is to find balance—or equanimity. This is the quality of nonreactive spaciousness that allows us to discern what's actually happening and then to respond in a skillful way.

I introduced this concept to the couple and we spent many sessions working to understand and then transform their entrenched pattern of negative reactivity. (This is also something that can happen in the workplace when, for example, any new idea from an employee reflexively receives a "no" from their risk-averse manager.) Couples often get into these patterns, and here I helped C and V get into one of attentive presence in, and for, each other's experience. This led to what Joseph Goldstein, the well-known author, teacher, and co-founder of Insight Meditation Society, calls "balanced compassion." Their equanimity even led to gratitude for the good times that had been so smothered by the weight of despair.

Expressing appreciation strengthened C and V's bond enough to find the courage to go deeper still—to get out from under the years of confusion, self-protection, and emotional separation so they could reflect on these questions:

- What is my most desired purpose or mission for myself?

- For my spouse?

- For our relationship?

- And for our family?

And when they shared their very thoughtful answers, they were surprised to learn that they were not that far apart in their mission. From these conversations, they were able to create a truly compassionate understanding of why they were together now, what they were doing to build a much healthier union, and how they could thrive individually, as a couple, and as a family. I was a witness to their drive to remain together and stay on track.

MISSION: THE CROSSOVER

In the work world, even for businesses founded on a clear purpose, it is important that they revisit their mission periodically for a variety of reasons. The exercise breathes fresh air into an established enterprise, gives the business a competitive advantage in the marketplace, and supports the leadership to focus on what means most to their diverse stakeholder group—shareholders, staff, customers, and community partners.

MISSION CASE STUDY: WORK

E and E, the co-owners of a 50-person organic food dis-
tribution business, needed to take a breath from the daily
hustle of the last five years and devote some time to this
revisiting. Their goals were threefold: to formally recom-
mit to the original mission, to ensure their present staff
were in alignment with it, and to identify ways that their
engagement could be enhanced.

Here is the definitional framework we used:

- A mission represents the fundamental reason for an
  organization's existence—their unique purpose.

- Another way of thinking of the mission: "What are we
  here to do together?"

The larger team was divided into cross-functional triads to
develop a draft of an overarching organizational mission
statement. I asked them to answer three very specific questions. And I encouraged them to use the experience they
had—leading different aspects of the business—to inform
their answers from their particular points of view:

1 **Why are we in business?** This challenged them to clarify
   the company's purpose, not to describe what it does, but
   why it does it and what outcomes it strives to achieve.

   "To create a sustainable planet ... to ensure people have
   healthy food to eat ... to partner with local food grow-
   ers in our community... to keep our environmental
   values alive ..."

2 **What business are we in?** This describes what the business does, the need or opportunity it fulfills, and the methods it uses to accomplish the purpose.

"Food delivery service... keeping families healthy... supporting farmers..."

3 **Who do we do it for?** Every business is serving some kind of customer, client, or stakeholder. And if it can't answer this question, why does the business even exist?

"Individuals... families... businesses... community..."

The triads came together to share their drafts and, with a bit of wordsmithing, they landed on a clear and inspiring statement of purpose. From that foundation, the room started to vibrate with scores of brilliant ideas on how to translate the team's purpose into action. Here, the mission was the *catalyst* for creative thinking and group empowerment.

There was some kind of magic in the air that day. The management team arrived full of curiosity and enthusiasm, keen to participate in the conversations about what mattered to them individually, as a team, and as an organization. E and E set the stage with their exceptional sensitivity and understanding of the group's mood and energy. Their emotional intelligence, proven business acumen, generosity, and open-minded welcome made clear their desire to really listen to all points of view. During the series of exercises, the team was invited to make meaningful contributions to their company, and they went for it. Their enthusiasm was almost uncontainable—creative, expansive ideas and opinions flowed from the working groups on how to enrich their customers' (and by extension their own) experience.

That's what happens when leaders like E and E give staff the chance to participate as true collaborators—they end up with far superior results. When we are really listened to, when our thoughts, feelings, and opinions count, then our confidence is boosted and we are propelled into action.

As a witness to this process many times over, I am enchanted. By offering employees the opportunity to have a voice in shaping their purpose at work, leaders give a double gift: they empower their staff to take action in their professional lives, and in their personal lives too. In shaping their purpose at work, they see the benefit in doing the same at home.

The result was a revised mission statement that stretched the team to grow their contribution to the community, get creative about deepening their customers' experience, and become more deliberate in engaging their staff in significant ways, day in and day out.

Mission statements don't have to be fancy or complicated. A small family-owned business I worked with told me that their mission was "to have fun, make tons of money, and give their customers the best entertainment experience in the city." That's it. If they stop enjoying what they do and don't make a profit, they will close it all down.

A mission is *sustaining*. In our demanding roles as team members and family members, we are constantly managing the precarious balance of work and home, being pushed and pulled by the needs and wants of the people in both those orbits. That's why having a clearly defined purpose can keep us present in all aspects of our lives, resilient and connected to ourselves and to each other. These are just some of the key benefits of a holistic approach to leadership.

HOME
WORK

Answer this question: Why are you and everyone else here?

Here is an example of a mission statement (from one of my own lines of business) based on the formula I set out above:

"I advise enterprising families [this is the *for whom* element] to maintain and grow their relational health [*what I do*] so they can increase their social impact and enjoy their financial health [*why I do it*]."

As a leader at work and/or at home, answer these questions to help you get in better touch with your mission:

- What are you most passionate about?
- What gives you a sense of meaningful purpose?
- Where does your power for living and leading come from?
- Name one action that you consistently take to put your passion, purpose, and power into being. Be specific!
- Who benefits from this in your personal life? In your professional life?

Now you have all the essential elements to write your own individual mission statement.

You can ask the same questions of your family members and your leadership team, and together develop these mission statements too.

VISION

Aspire toward a
Compelling Future

GREAT LEADERS ARE NOT
PROVERBIAL FENCE-SITTERS.
THEY JUDGE. THEY OPINE.
THEY CHALLENGE. THEY
FIGHT FOR THEIR VISION.

GAD SAAD

ENVISIONING THE FUTURE state of a system that seeks continuity will allow it to grow. It's not enough for our families and workplaces to have a core mission and shared values. We also need to manage and adapt to the changes that will inevitably occur, both incremental and radical. This doesn't mean that we abandon our enduring character or shift our ideology, but without a vision we can get stuck in old operating patterns that can turn the system inward, immovable, and ultimately ineffective. And it can be boring!

I invite people to take a trip to Possibility Land, a place where the doors to imagining future options are always open so that our minds can be open too. It's a bold journey for many because it can feel overwhelming rather than expansive. "Can't I just keep doing what I'm doing? Why do I need to think about the future? Why set a plan when I know I can't/won't/don't keep to it?" And even if you are open to the idea of aspiring to more, it's common to get caught in the "yes, but ..." mindset of envisioning a future state: "I want to become a more patient parent, but I'm just like my mother and she could never relax," or "We need to reach a more global market, but it's too risky," or "Our family business could adopt a transgenerational vision, but all our conversations now end in a fight."

Imagining our home and work lives beyond our day-to-day activities takes courage. I've seen many families and leadership teams turn this visioning exercise into an inspiring adventure, uncovering the big picture possibilities for their respective systems. Creating a vision of our future helps us figure out what we want to achieve, how we can stretch our abilities and become part of something much larger than ourselves. A compelling vision gives shape, focus, and direction to the changes we want to make and the dreams we want to realize. And figuring this all out together makes for deeper understanding and a more resilient and integrated system.

VISION CASE STUDY: HOME

Over the last decade, a number of couples *preparing* for marriage have reached out for my counseling services. They are motivated to create the conditions for future marital success (and more than the occasional moments of bliss). Without exception, these couples are paying a very high psychic tax—the price of their respective families' expectations and traditions around The Wedding. Even if their vision of the ceremony is different than that of their families', they are compelled by desire, guilt, fear, custom, or confusion to please.

I invite people to take a trip to Possibility Land, where the doors are always open so that our minds can be open too.

At best, this can temporarily destabilize the couple's agency to create their milestone event. Heightened emotions and divided loyalties threaten their ability to discern between their own needs and everyone else's. At worst, this could set up a dangerous dynamic between them and their families of origin. Whose marriage is this anyway? What boundaries are precipitously challenged even before the wedding happens? Deciding to marry is an act of deep conviction. Wise couples realize that marriage is about building "a future together" (not just having a party), and that it necessitates a coming together of their collective vision. Visioning is a way to clarify a path to a successful union right from the start. Here's how N and MJ, a young engaged couple, did just that.

Both were at an age and stage of readiness to fully connect and commit. They quickly settled into the warm glow of a serious relationship full of respect, fun, and promise. After a successful two-year courtship, they decided to marry.

N and MJ were not unaware of the inherent challenges in every union. Both were witness to their parents' terrible divorces, and many of their friends had split up with too much rancor and malice. Others were living in strikingly indifferent situations that seemed even worse. And as they were planning their wedding, the forces (and typical intrusions) from their respective families—the choice of officiate, who makes the invitation list, how many bridesmaids, the parental posturing and pouting—were diverting their attention and interfering in their connection. Despite all this and the recognition of no guarantees in their future wedded bliss, they were still full of hope.

In preparation, N and MJ decided to seek out pre-marital counseling to design their relationship vision. Their aim was to draw an aspirational yet achievable picture of the marriage they wanted to create. They didn't shy away from the courageous conversations I facilitated about the trifecta of trouble many couples encounter in long-term relationships: sex, money, and child-raising. The couple realized their foundational beliefs about money—saving over spending—were the same, but they had differences in terms of *when* to start saving; essentially, they were traveling at different speeds. Child-rearing quickly focused in on religion, where they had different ideas about how or if religion should take a place in raising kids. But here it is interesting to note that N and MJ also had different visions around *when* they thought they might start trying for a family, and so the tensions around religion were really a proxy for the differences in how quickly they each wanted to commit their lives to parenting (and say goodbye to uninterrupted sex for many years!). This conversation, facilitated by an objective and nonjudgmental professional, gave them both the permission and the courage to open up in a way that was safe and less likely to spiral out of control. As they entered into their union with more intimate information, confidence, energy, and presence, N and MJ knew they had begun to build an even stronger bond and a more solid foundation.

VISION: THE CROSSOVER

Aspiration for future success is also a task for leaders of family businesses. By definition, these complex systems combine the high emotion of the relational with the necessary discipline of the professional. They also take a long-term view, honoring the core vision established by the founders and then re-visioning their future states to ensure continuity. This is one of the many paradoxes these kinds of businesses have to manage: tradition and change.

VISION CASE STUDY: FAMILY BUSINESS

"From shirtsleeves to shirtsleeves in three generations" is an old adage in the family business world. In essence, it describes how common it is for family-owned firms to fail by the time their ownership reaches the third generation. Unfortunately, the statistics bear this out. Approximately 30 percent of family-owned firms survive or remain in the family from the first to the second generation. Only 10 percent of them continue into the third generation.[21] That's why this story of a family enterprise that celebrated its 100-year anniversary is so rare and inspiring.

What a milestone, a feat of persistence and dedication! It has somehow adapted to the shifting family cultures across four generations to successfully build a legacy. How have they managed to stay together? I think it is because of their strongly shared "moral imagination"—a principle that is actually deeper and more powerful than a typical vision statement. Wesley and Robles in "The Power of

Family Culture" describe this concept as "the development of the heartfelt and creative collective calling that puts the family in relationship to one another and with the promise of its own future in community."[22]

Many of the stories the descendants tell about Z, their great-grandfather, describe his commitment to continuity. When Z arrived from Romania as a poor young man of 18, he dreamt of being his own boss and building a lasting legacy for his future family. He labored 18 hours a day to get his business in the rag trade (*shmata* in Yiddish) off the ground, only stopping for the Sabbath. He met his wife R in a tiny synagogue where other Jewish immigrants worshipped, and she had the same desire for family continuity (what we professionally refer to as a "legacy family" story). As R would say to her husband and children: "Why not make it last for the next five generations?"

This turned into a running joke, for it seemed so impossible that this little sewing factory could sustain them at all. But their faith, deep drive, and moral imagination guided their actions and kept their vision strong. It was never a question that the kids would work anywhere but in their parents' business. The same "rule" applied for the grandkids and now the great-grandkids. Their cross-generational interdependence and engagement became the glue that kept the family authentic and aligned, and the business whole.

The changes they have managed across the century have been enormous—in growth, leadership style, technology, and manufacturing to name just a few. And they've been able to stay true to their original traditions. One hundred years later, that little factory has become a major force in the women's wear industry. They have made a significant difference in the world through their philanthropy, continue to raise mostly contented and emotionally healthy children, and are still focused on the long view. Z and R's multigenerational family business dream has turned from a comic fantasy into a sincere and shared reality.

Visions are regenerative, not reductive. Articulating a vision is fundamental to developing a high-performing team or a healthy and harmonious family. It's the vision that can motivate and focus us to expand our horizons and reach our goals.

VISION: THE APPROACH

When I work with organizations or families to create their vision, I invest a great deal of energy and time in exploring where they want to go. And they need to want to get there together; it never works when a leader imposes the future state. Participative discovery and collaboration, albeit a sometimes-grueling endeavor, can turn possibilities into a clear picture of the future we want to create for our homes, workplaces, and the communities we wish to impact.

Here is the framework I use with work and family teams who are in the vision discovery process:

- A vision is the picture of our future we seek.

- It answers the question "What do we want to strive to create in the future within an agreed-upon time frame?"

- The vision informs your mission, which in turn drives your plan to achieve it.

Ideally, the vision will have these characteristics:

- It is something you are *striving* for—it's a stretch but it's achievable.

- It has to *excite and inspire* you.

- It should *challenge* you, both your beliefs and your paradigms.

- It should clearly describe a state of the "preferred future."

- It must reflect your *values*, so that you are wholly committed to its achievement no matter what it takes.

- It must be *communicated* so that it is pervasive in your life.

The questions I ask leadership teams and family groups in order to activate their visioning hearts and minds are different now than they were earlier in my career. They take into consideration the accelerated pace of change today—not only the technology that is transforming our workplaces and homes, but also the political, social, environmental, and economic drivers that affect the possibilities for the systems we want to realize. Therefore, we shorten the time frame to increase the vision's achievability. Of course, imagining the future continuity of a business, a family, or a family firm is ideal, but it can also cause anxiety and even complacency. We want a vision to be clear and deliberate, so it can be actionably pursued and attained by the members of the system.

Here's a springboard exercise I often use to help my clients get started on crafting their vision statement. I ask them to "imagine reading an article about your company or family five or ten years into the future that describes its achievements. What does the headline say?" Here are a couple of examples:

> "Successful National Family Business Transitions into 3rd Generation Ownership"

> "Two Healthy Kids and the Romance Is Still Alive!"

We can get so caught up in the present (the *doing* of our work and home lives) or the past (regretting what we haven't done) that we can easily lose sight of the future possibilities for *being*. Articulating an aspiration for our future selves can compel us to discover potential we never dared to dream of.

HOME
WORK

Ask yourself this question: What do you want to become?

In your role as a leader, try to create your own vision statement. Remember to shorten the time frame to the next 3–5 years. Here are a few examples from clients to get you thinking:

> "To make the best decisions, I will become an invitational leader and welcome my team's opinions, thoughts, and suggestions."

> "Less fear, more boldness."

> "I will create a strong and lasting family business by developing excellent professional relationships with my children, nieces and nephews who work with me. I will be a loving mentor!"

Here are a few things to keep in mind before you start:

1 Keep it simple. And brief.

2 Focus on what kind of leader you want to become, and think about those specific actions, traits, experiences, and competencies that would have a significant impact on your leadership in the future.

3 Be positive and say what you want to become. This is a "yes" statement, so try to find positive alternatives to any negative language.

4 Create a statement that will guide you in your everyday actions and decisions as a leader. Yes, it should be aspirational, but bring it down to earth so you can take steps to make it achievable.

5 If the language is emotional, it will give you more energy and compel you to more action. Don't hold back.

You are creating a living document. Once you have a "good-enough" draft, communicate it to your stakeholders, live with it for a while, and use it to keep yourself energized. Then keep refining it as your leadership evolves.

STRATEGY

Make a Plan and Set the Goals to Achieve It

THE THING ABOUT GOALS IS
THAT LIVING WITHOUT THEM IS
A LOT MORE FUN, IN THE SHORT
RUN. IT SEEMS TO ME, THOUGH,
THAT THE PEOPLE WHO GET
THINGS DONE, WHO LEAD, WHO
GROW, WHO MAKE AN IMPACT...
THOSE PEOPLE HAVE GOALS.

SETH GODIN

WHEN I THINK of the common business practice of strategic planning, I imagine leaders' top shelves littered with thick volumes of outdated plans, covered with the dust and detritus of their best intentions.

In principle, having a big-picture organizational strategy is an important and worthwhile focus for executives, but it doesn't always translate into a successful reality. Many leaders are encouraged to spend huge amounts of money (consultancy fees) and time (focus groups, interviews, surveys, more focus groups, higher consultancy fees) developing complex, lengthy, and detailed three-, five-, and ten-year strategic plans for their organizations. But the speed of change is head-spinning, rendering these sweeping prognostications and deliberations quickly redundant, inadequate, or just plain wrong.

On the home front, families are constantly making plans—albeit in less institutionalized and formal ways—for having and then raising children; for the unparalleled summer holiday; for making, spending, and saving money;

and for fighting against relationship entropy and the gradual decline of desire that can often happen in long-term relationships, just to name a few.

We like to plan. In fact, we are compelled to—if for no other reason than to stave off the incontrovertible fact that we really have no control over the future. Over my decades of practice, there are some persistent truths about human nature I have been taught by my clients in support of this view:

1   We have an angst-ridden aversion to not knowing what's going to happen.

2   We want to eliminate the possible risks of something bad happening at home and at work.

3   We try to manage the uncertainty and fear by setting strategy and making plans.

4   Unsurprisingly, we overestimate our ability to predict the future, yet hold an unstinting optimism to keep on planning.

What else are we going to do if we want to fulfill our purpose and achieve the vision of our most desired future state? I actually don't know of many companies or families who want to be complacent or static or stuck. But what I *have* noticed is that although being proactive and having a growth mindset are seen as absolute imperatives for businesses, families tend to be more reactive; things "happen" to families, where there doesn't seem to be even the illusion of agency.

Leaders need the resilience to **live outside the comfort zone** of certainty.

We can change that. When the conversations get to a deeper level, I learn that my clients want to set their sights further ahead. They are sometimes anxious about the ambiguity of possible paths, for sure, but they nevertheless want and need to propel themselves forward in some coherent way. Whether their motivation for developing a plan is internal or driven by external change, organizational and family systems require both a discipline and a roadmap to allow for successful and healthy continuity.

So I'm not at all arguing for a total erasure of planning. But I am suggesting that leaders practice discernment, keep the strategies simple and sensible, and recognize that it's not about perfection. We can benefit from reducing the time frame, and not holding too tightly to a precise result.

The theorist Henry Mintzberg distinguished between "deliberate" and "emergent" strategy-making, reasoning that planners cannot be too intentional, but must be responsive to a variety of unanticipated events in their ecosystem.[23] For leaders to increase their odds of success, they need the resilience to live outside the comfort zone of certainty. They must encourage and engage their teams to figure out what they want to achieve, and then assess whether it's reasonable to even try.

I believe this absolutely applies to our home lives as well. The anxiety of uncertainty can be the precursor to chaos. Here's a story about a family struck by tragedy that had no strategy and no plan, just the fierce cascades of loss and fear for the ones who were left to grieve.

STRATEGY CASE STUDY: HOME

H was golden, beloved by his family, friends, business community, and anyone who ever met him. All of a sudden, he had a heart attack and died in the middle of a work meeting. Because H was so young and fit, there was no preparation for his passing. I've heard from many family members that whether they lose a loved one fast or slow, both endings are devastating. The loss that ripped through H's world had everyone flailing. He left a bereft wife and two very young children, but not too young to be immune to the damage his untimely death triggered. At an age that's normally a formative time of developing healthy relationships and the ability to cope with life's ups and downs, losing a parent made it so much harder for these tender hearts and minds.

Not surprisingly, everyone in the family system was showing signs of trauma. For the children, obsessive worry about their mother T's safety and fear of her imminent death, night terrors and insomnia, disordered eating, inability to concentrate in school, and acting out. For T, manic episodes of over-functioning to keep it all together and debilitating periods of depression and anxiety. The air was thick with dread and the family system became closed off to the world, separated by T's inability to ask for help. At least there was a healthy insurance policy and enough savings.

The first year was one of survival. I met T after that, when she was ready to reach out for support. She wanted to move from just surviving to living a more psychologically stable, actively engaged, and available life with her kids. Coping with the absence of a lover, co-parent, and friend was slightly less debilitating by then, but her family needed a different kind of attention, even reconstruction. As the leader, T was determined to set them all on a path to well-being.

One of the things I've learned over the years is how parents always put themselves last, mothers especially. When I asked T to list what she was most concerned with—what she wanted to focus on—she said it was the physical and emotional well-being of her seven-year-old twins, their school experience, and expanding their friend group. When I asked her where *she* was on the list, her response was one of surprise. It didn't actually occur to T that she could get on that list too. So we did just that. We began our conversations to answer these questions:

- What did she want for her son and daughter?

- What did she want for herself?

- What did they want from her?

From there T determined her strategy. For the next year, her family would be on a one-foot-in-front-of-the-other journey to recover from H's death, to rebuild the foundation of their family without him, and to celebrate more than a few moments of true joy. That's it. When a family has been in shock and crisis like theirs had, you can't be too ambitious. The fragility of the system needs to be respected so it doesn't become flooded with the thick fear of expectations unrealized, of the uncontrollable unknown.

And because this is a system, it needs a leader to navigate it. Here, the leader is T. And as the leader, she will need to set some goals to strengthen the psychological, emotional, and relational terrain of her tribe:

- That her children will receive her present attention by offering daily signs of recognition and love from their surviving parent, in words and actions, to remind them they matter.

- That the family will receive therapy once a month to have a safe place to work on the 3 Cs of the family relationship: communication, cohesiveness, and conflict management. (The right strategy is to help them find age-appropriate ways to move through and manage the confusing and negative emotions like anger, fear, resentment, and hurt.)

- That T will become a parent aide at the school and learn tools to support the kids to develop their studying skills.

- That the family will invite their extended "supporters" (grandparents, aunts, uncles, cousins, and close friends) to play a more active and ongoing role in their pathway to healing... dinners, playdates, late-night crying calls, celebrations, and so on.

- That T will reserve one evening each week to reconnect with herself to find pleasure and purpose in whatever ways feel safe and nourishing—meet a friend, go to a movie, take a class, read a book, do a little retail therapy—any action to build her resilience and manage her mental health.

The best strategy for recovering after a tragic family event is meaningful engagement in relationships, a co-regulation process that calms the nervous systems of the family members and strengthens their individual and collective resilience. Fostering dialogue and harnessing the support of the whole system of resources is the most natural form of healing from the loss they experienced. When this family was able to actively share their vulnerability with each other and their extended network, there was a flow of generosity, care, and nurturance to the bereaved. In grieving together, they healed together.

STRATEGY: THE CROSSOVER

In the world of work, developing a strategic plan for an organization or business relies on an entire, and often confusing, nomenclature. There is a prolific lexicon of terms that are used interchangeably, depending on which expert's methodology or latest transformational process you choose. There are "themes," "directions," "factors," "priorities," and "platforms" to determine. There are "objectives," "strategies," "tactics," "initiatives," "goals," "targets," and "actions" to establish. So we have to wind our way through all the jargon while simultaneously trying to gain control of the future of our business or family. Who wouldn't want to run from the task?

I don't have a blithe disregard for all the rules and protocols of strategic planning, but I do want to offer my clients clarity and remove the confusion they often feel in their journeys. As a result—and in order to reduce the pressure—I've streamlined my process, and introduce only a few simple guidelines and terms. Since leaders are grounded in their mission and directed by their vision, they already know what they do and for whom. Because they've determined their company's desired future state, they know where they want to be. Now leaders need a plan to get there. My job is to help them and their teams to focus on making choices about which stakeholders to target and how to create value for them. Once that is clear, they can develop a plan to address their strategic challenges.

STRATEGY CASE STUDY: WORK

Here's a story about a team at a small but mighty company in the recycling sector that were "strat planning" neophytes. They didn't have the resources to take on an elaborate and costly exercise, so they wanted an abridged approach and process. They were astute enough to understand that their vision might need some calibration but were confident they could consider a timeline of 12–24 months to achieve it. The president was one of the most driven leaders I've ever met and her leadership team was full of creativity. They wanted an external facilitator to hold the container for all the energy and get them started.

The team had already spent time understanding their three target stakeholders: customers, suppliers, and employees. Here is a very useful question to find out what is in the way—or out of the way—when putting together a strategy around stakeholders: What do you want from them, and what do they want from you?

Here, I encouraged the team to avoid focusing on the way things had always been, on how they had always "understood" the wants and needs of their stakeholders, but never really challenged those beliefs. We brainstormed the directions the company could take in the next 1–2 years to address the changing needs of those stakeholders, and quickly came up with over a dozen strategies. What was revealing is that this work clearly mattered to them: they worried over each strategy like a favorite child and wrestled with choosing the most important ones. In the end, the team did a fine job of collaborating to fine-tune their list down to the three most significant and urgent strategies. They were as follows:

1   Deepen customer experience.

2   Engage employees.

3   Increase operational efficiencies.

The next step was to create realistic goals for each strategy and to assign a leader to be accountable for achieving them. Because they weren't tied to a looming years-long plan, the leaders could be nimble enough to change direction if they realized they were focused on the wrong thing, or if radical shifts in their external environment took place. And then they really got to work.

Setting goals is harder than it seems. "Increasing profitability" is too broad and makes people anxious. "Being happy at work" is too hard to define, since happiness will mean very different things for each employee.

You've likely heard of the SMART acronym. It's an easy-to-remember framework that's essentially a formula for turning a wish into a goal. Here's a quick overview:

- **S is specific.** Clearly define your goal and avoid being vague. Lack of clarity leads to distraction and confusion.

- **M is measurable.** Track your progress by identifying milestones, or you'll lose your motivation.

- **A is achievable.** Sure, you want to challenge and maybe even stretch everyone's abilities, but keep your goals realistic enough so you don't become overwhelmed and discouraged.

- **R is relevant.** Every goal you set must be related to and in alignment with your mission, vision, and values. If it's not, then why bother wasting your time, energy, and resources?

- **T is timely.** Goals without a deadline can go on forever. You set them from a sense of urgency, so by definition it's a need, not simply a desire. Name a time frame and stick to it.

Here's a template to help you get SMART in focusing your goals:

That:	**Your Stakeholder/Member/Client**
Has/have received:	**A Product/Service/Information**
By:	**Deadline/Due Date**
In order to:	**Advance your vision and/or mission**

And here are a few examples from the recycling company's story:

Strategy: Deepen customer experience.

Goal: That all **new and existing customers** receive a full **recycling audit and an updated program design** for their home or business within the **next 6 months** to further **reduce their waste and increase our bottom line.**

Strategy: Engage employees.

Goal: That **all employees** receive **training and certification** in the new e-waste technology by **September 30** (the end of fiscal year, or F/Y) in order to become an **employer of choice** in our industry and **increase our customer offerings.**

Strategy: Increase operational efficiencies.

Goal: That the **end user** will have access to an **online booking system** to schedule and confirm pickup days and times by the **end of Q2** to **reduce human error** and **wasted time and costs.**

The more specific the goal, the likelier you'll achieve it.

Once the SMART goals are defined, they can be broken down into action plans. Start at the beginning and detail how long each step will take, and therefore when it will be complete, before using that as the starting date for the next stage. If a specific date is already fixed for the final deadline and can't be moved, use that as the starting point and project the timeline for each stage backwards to calculate when the first stage needs to start. If you've already passed the projected start date, some stages will need to be rethought to make an achievable plan (for instance, by increasing the number of staff assigned to them). The following example uses the employee goal given above.

Goal: That all employees receive training and certification in the new e-waste technology by September 30 (the end of F/Y) in order to become an employer of choice in our industry and increase our customer offerings.

1 **Task:** Training and certification programs researched, cost–benefit analysis completed, and recommendations for CEO prepared.
   Assigned to: Training Coordinator.
   Deadline: January 30.

2 **Task:** Vendor chosen and employee communication detailing initiative and rationale completed.
   Assigned to: CEO, with support from Communication Coordinator.
   Deadline: February 15.

3 **Task:** Training schedules set and participants notified.
   Assigned to: Training coordinator.
   Deadline: February 28.

4 **Task:** Training begins.
   Assigned to: Training coordinator.
   Deadline: March 15.

5 **Task:** Monthly follow-up with vendor and participants, with bimonthly updates to SMT.
   Assigned to: Training coordinator.
   Deadline: SMT meetings on 15th of each month (April and July).

6   **Task:** All participants certified in the new technology.
    Assigned to: Participants.
    Deadline: September 15.

7   **Task:** Company-wide celebration and communication.
    Assigned to: Communication Coordinator + speakers.
    Deadline: September 30.

Too detailed? Too bad! Without a list of comprehensive actions, your goals, albeit SMART-ly defined, can't be achieved. You can read this as an overly prescribed process but do it anyway, because this is how the strategies come to life and the systems succeed within the uncertainty.

HOME
WORK

Ask yourself this question: How are you going to achieve your goals?

1   Define a strategy you would like to implement that would help you get closer to realizing your vision (personal, corporate, team, or family).

Remember this personal vision example? "To make the best decisions, I will become an invitational leader and welcome my team's opinions, thoughts, and suggestions." To translate that intention into action, the strategy could be as simple as "engage my staff."

2   Using the formula in this lesson, try to define one SMART goal you will need to accomplish for your strategy.

So, to accomplish your strategy of engaging your staff, one of your goals can be "that the leadership team has a rigorous and consistent communication and collaboration process with the CEO [you!] in order to get to the best decisions."

3   Then use the action plan template above to determine the steps you will need to take in order to achieve your own goal.

GOVERNANCE

Create a Safe Container

EFFECTIVE GOVERNANCE
CAN BE DEFINED AS CREATING
PROCESSES THAT MAKE
REVOLUTION UNNECESSARY.

CRAIG ARONOFF AND JOHN WARD

GOVERNANCE, BROADLY DEFINED, consists of three things:

1. How groups are managed.
2. How power is exercised.
3. How accountability is established.

For me, good governance is like the nerve center of healthy communication and decision-making at work and at home. The quote by Aronoff and Ward above is my favorite description of the concept. It goes without saying that family business systems are inherently more tender emotional terrains than your average workplace, but governance practices still apply and can help to regulate emotions and reduce disequilibrium and disharmony. Regardless of the setting, when leaders institute and employ governance tools, they can transform closed, chaotic, and divisive systems into more trusting, transparent, and harmonious ones.

I've rarely met a leader who remains untouched by **the impact of their authority** on the people they like and love.

Good governance can prevent emotion from wreaking havoc. I know that sounds a bit dramatic, but when people with differing opinions and stakes come together without a clear and safe container to communicate effectively (even fiercely) and get to the right decisions, it can create an explosive cocktail of resentment, wrong assumptions, and systemic dysfunction.

I believe leaders try hard to be both benevolent and responsible communicators and effective decision-makers. But they are real people, not neutral players without skin in the game. This is where the leadership quality of self-knowledge really kicks into high gear. They must recognize and manage their own internal dynamics: ego, insecurities, ethics, complicated histories, and the vicissitudes of their personal and professional relationships. Then they have to navigate the reactions and experiences of those affected by their decisions.

This requires managing relationships. I've rarely met a leader who remains untouched by the impact of their authority on the people they like and love, which is perhaps why some leaders have such a hard time clearly communicating, making tough decisions, and then ensuring that they stick.

The difficulties inherent in decision-making are ubiquitous in both work and family systems. Here are the six most vexing challenges experienced by leaders I've supported:

1 Determining and then accepting where the authority should lie. Too often the role of decision-maker is assumed but not formalized. Organizational and family

politics can make the situation more unclear, so the deciders can shift depending on who's holding the power.

2 Ensuring the decision-makers have the expertise and ability they need to responsibly wield that power. Positional power-holders aren't always qualified to make the best decisions, especially when they don't have the information, the emotional intelligence, and the respect of the group to do so.

3 Embracing the role of decider and being held accountable for seeing the choices through. Reluctant leadership is all too common in work and family cultures where the pressure to be inclusive, empowering, and collaborative is intense. Also, leaders who are conflict-avoidant have trouble making decisions and so when they do, their decisions are half-hearted and not properly managed.

4 Balancing the need to control (the business, the family, the community) with welcoming the participation of those who will be impacted (employees, family members) by the decisions taken. For some leaders, relinquishing control is difficult and sometimes even inconceivable! They pay lip service to others' opinions but in the end it's "my way or the highway." (For the reluctant leaders, they ask for everyone's feedback and too easily abandon their own point of view.)

5 Making hard and courageous choices and practicing acts of compassion all at once. Think about laying off staff, terminating a family member who works

in the business, or practicing "tough love" with a substance-abusing adult child. Cultivating and actually putting these two leadership qualities—courage and compassion—into practice when the stakes are high is a monumental challenge.

6   Proactively developing processes, structures, and policies before problems brew and crises lead to revolution. In fact, the main reason clients call me is because they *didn't* put any governance in place and it's five … ten … even twenty years later and the system is in chaos. Many first meetings begin with "We should have gotten professional help a long time ago."

To manage these complex challenges, there are many different governance tools for leaders at home and at work to develop that will promote unity and commitment while getting things done, like running a business or raising a family. These tools offer safety, metaphorically and literally. I create a "contained" atmosphere for my clients where they can have honest conversations to determine the rules of engagement to keep the system healthy. And the systems and processes themselves are specific enough so that everyone understands who does what, and why.

GOVERNANCE CASE STUDY: HOME

In this story of a family caught in a precarious battle for authority, I worked with the parents to create a safe container to hold their power, build clear generational boundaries, and ultimately improve their relationships with their child and each other.

No one was sure who was inflicting more pain and suffering on whom: the parents, who were trying in vain to manage an out-of-control child, or the child whose willfulness could not be thwarted. B and F identified their daughter, A, as the problem (and the patient) and they wanted someone (me) to fix her. It's a big risk for parents who feel vulnerable and even a bit ashamed to come for treatment. They were victims to all the "shoulds" of parenting, and were beset by a growing sense of failure and inability to fulfill the expectations that their families, friends, and the whole parenting culture placed upon them. Parents are under enormous pressure to be instant experts at childrearing, familiar with the latest and greatest theories and techniques, and able to manage every situation with calmness and clarity. Even though they knew these impossible expectations couldn't be met, B and F still felt beaten down. I needed to learn more about how they arrived at feeling so lost, and asked them to share their experiences.

"She came out screaming," F began, and I didn't know if he meant literally at A's birth, or if this was the father's shorthand for how the parents thought about her character from the start. Indeed, they meant that right from the

start they were overwhelmed with the awesome responsibility of their new role. B and F were more than a little
bit scared of this powerful being. Where was the owner's
manual?! There were many sleepless nights and breath-
less days, trying to make sense of A's behavior and all the
advice everyone threw at them. They just wanted her to be
a "good baby." As she grew into a little girl, A's stubborn-
ness would flare like a fire and then dissolve into a quiet
peace. These periods of relief gave the family a sense of
what "regular" could feel like. Still, most of the time was
spent managing the moody and shifting landscapes of her
childhood. B and F vacillated between exhausted resigna-
tion and desperate, unaligned attempts to control. They
felt that they had "tried everything," but listening to their
struggles, it was easy to see some very common patterns:
They coddled A—a very familiar dynamic in contempo-
rary culture—but the way they described it was odd in that
they seemed somewhat proud of it. They communicated
mixed messages around "acceptable conduct"—but what
was revealing is that they focused on A's conduct, and not
the inconsistencies around their own behavioral patterns
as parents. And of course, there was a lot of frustration
around boundaries. Here, B and F felt absolutely immobi-
lized. And further conversation revealed that at the most
basic level, they were insecure about power—what power
they should impose on A, and what power they even felt
confident in imposing should they choose to.

Ultimately, the kid was running the family show.
As the brilliant psychotherapist Andrew Feldmar once
told me, "If anyone needs to be a monster, it cannot be

the child," and A was mastering monstrous behavior to great effect.

And here's where systems come in: A secondary but not insignificant consequence of the unending parenting stresses was the couple's disintegrating relationship. They had no energy for it. Their communication focused on updates, schedule changes, or litanies of complaints met with silence or loud defiance. Their best selves were saved for their child, not for each other.

As is often the case in families without clear parent-child boundaries, A—already a very intuitive little girl—was becoming an expert manipulator and, frankly, an effective decision-maker. She was proficient at triangulation, often refusing to communicate directly with her mom, and forcing her dad to be the messenger of A's many demands. And then she'd do the same with the other parent, creating deeper fissures between the beleaguered couple and essentially reorganizing the adult relationship. But monsters are made, not born. It was time for B and F to reverse the power dynamic and reset the family pattern before it was too late.

I booked the first set of sessions in their home so that I could understand their particular kind of messiness. In order to make any intervention, I had to enter their environment and experience their family dynamic in real time. Joining their system as a kind of participant-observer, I was able to gain knowledge and credibility by asking a lot of questions, ensuring everyone had the opportunity to share their experiences and feelings, act as a translator between the family members to increase understanding, and help them manage their strong emotions in the sessions through co-regulating techniques to calm down their nervous systems. Gradually I was able to create a safe container, engage everyone, and help them to solve their family problem. This systemic process removed the "identified patient" label from A and empowered all family members to be part of the solution. Our family sessions allowed me to see how the relationship patterns played out, and how those interactions might be shifted toward more healthy and functional forms. Metaphorically, we were in a process of changing the steps of their family dance.

Working on the adult relationship was a parallel step. I reminded B and F that they were the leaders of their family. Up until now, they had never really talked about their authority as parents because they were caught in a cycle of reacting to each challenge and its ensuing crisis without any mutual understanding or agreement on how to proceed. I watched them do it over and over again. F would acquiesce to A's fourth request for another cartoon right after everyone agreed to a limit of three before bed. B would start screaming when the child started screaming, and then F would just walk out the door and abandon his assigned role as Calmer-in-Chief. So I asked: What were their values for parenting? How could they translate those into specific parenting behaviors? How could they be lovingly supportive of their daughter while owning their power and sticking to their decisions? Many heated and uncomfortable conversations later, they could unclench from their intractability and open to empathy, and eventually, to compassion. B and F found enough common ground to gradually put some governance tools in place.

- They established these Rules of Engagement on how to parent together:

  1 **Turn down the volume.** We find the emotional self-management to not lose our tempers and raise our voices. Breathing helps.

  2 **Discuss, don't react.** We take a stance of curiosity, not judgment. We ask a lot of questions to seek understanding.

  3 **Present a united front no matter what.** If we don't agree, we "put a pin in it" and work out our differences in private.

  4 **Set clear boundaries.** We never forget that we are the parents and she is the child, and we are in charge.

  5 **Lead with love.** Even if we don't always like what she's doing, our love for our daughter is unconditional.

- They had Sunday Night Family Meetings to talk about the past week and to offer loving recognition. Each meeting started with highlights and lowlights and things to do differently. They set family goals and worked through differences rather than explode, ignore, or acquiesce like they had in the past.

- B and F introduced rules of behavior called What's Okay (owning your feelings and expressing them, asking for a "time-out") and What's Not (yelling, name-calling, interrupting), and real consequences if they weren't followed.

- Using a collection of guided meditation recordings specifically designed for children, they began Family Mindfulness sessions for 5–10 minutes every night before A's bedtime.

- The parents committed to a weekly Date Night. Their psychic and emotional separation needed time to heal if they wanted a "romance rebirth." Spending dedicated couple time and a chance to discover each other as love partners could serve as a much-needed corrective and even a positive adventure.

It was rough at the start. A—no surprise—was wholly uninterested in this new dynamic and challenged their authority for the first few months of the new "regime." But to the extent that B and F firmly held to their rules, boundaries, and decisions, A eventually had to adapt and accept the new family rituals and routines. As her behavior regulated and her acceptance grew, the parents were able to unclench from their intractability and become more compassionate people. They had secured the family container by changing the relational patterns through instituting appropriate governance tools and techniques.

GOVERNANCE: THE CROSSOVER

In the working world, businesses that are well-governed are more effective in meeting their goals of maximizing profits and serving all their stakeholders. They often have boards of external directors or advisors to provide organizational oversight and stewardship of the company. And they have senior teams with clear roles and relationships to lead the organization. As a consequence, they are able to apply formal structures, processes, and policies to address a host of business imperatives—including contracts, regulations, human resources, asset management, talent management . . . the list goes on and on, but in a business of a sufficient size and level of professionalism, the protocols for handling all these operations are usually in place. But in family-owned and -operated firms, it's often a different story. The complexity in negotiating those corporate imperatives, alongside the interpersonally loaded and highly emotional relationships between family members, can be challenging to the point of overwhelming. And this really gets to the heart of why governance is such a nightmare (and that is not hyperbole) in family businesses; it's why the majority of these firms are so hesitant to introduce and implement good governance principles and tools.

Through a lot of hard lessons, I have seen how these guidelines—when appropriately and flexibly designed to fit the size, context, and personality of the business family—can effectively build commitment and trust, and engender successful stewardship. Conversely, without basic governance in place, I've witnessed deep family conflict, jealousies, power struggles, and an ambient animosity that poisons the system from one generation to the next. This can be particularly crippling for a family enterprise.

I try to get my clients on a solid, achievable governance path right away, even if it's just to create a simple organizational structure and clarify family, business, and ownership roles for each family member. These "rules" create the conditions for clear communication and better decision-making. They also decrease the risk of their businesses failing and their relationships being destroyed. Unfortunately, this happens much too often, leading to a heartbreaking and more-often-than-not preventable conclusion. Here's a story of how good governance can save a family firm.

GOVERNANCE CASE STUDY: FAMILY BUSINESS

Two entrepreneurial-minded brothers, G and Q, founded a manufacturing parts and service business after university, naturally taking on roles that reflected both their individual talents and abilities to meet the company's needs. As co-presidents, they worked closely and collaboratively to grow the company into one of the top five businesses in their region. G was brilliant at several roles: growing the client base year after year, building strong customer relationships, and being the external face of the company. Q—managing operations—was a master of financial planning, project management, and keeping their talented workforce engaged and empowered. They were a highly effective leadership/ownership team with complementary styles and skills.

They were also a close-knit family. Their wives were not only sisters-in-law but best friends, and their five children were brought up together—same schools, same church, same shared love of team sports, rock music, and each other. All the cousins helped out in the shop and the office after school, and three worked summer jobs for the company during their high school years. G and Q already treated their staff like family, so having the kids around was a natural extension of the culture. The founders were well-respected in their community and treated like small-town celebrities. They liked the status and wanted the same respect for their kids and grandkids... some day.

When the three cousins most active in the company expressed interest in joining full-time after they completed their education, the two sets of parents met to discuss how this could work. All agreed that family harmony was as much a priority as maintaining the business. They talked about how their relationship as brothers and business partners had been solid, with hardly any effort or formal governance structures in place except for a basic share-holder agreement. The 2008 downturn had taken a toll on the business, and they had made a few bad deals during their tenure, but overall, they were resilient and recovered handily. The business continued to thrive. Always able to hash out their differences and make decisions that were discerning rather than reactive, G and Q never ended a workday angry. They were instinctively collaborative in their drive for success. But would that leadership style automatically transfer to the rising generation? Not likely. The two couples decided that hoping for the same dynamic between their kids was too risky.

Governance: Approach

To manage the complexities of the family enterprise and prepare for the next generation's *formal* entry into the business was a heavy lift. The founder-couples invited me in to start the continuity planning conversation. We talked about how the overlapping circles of family, business, and ownership could get confusing, and I introduced some proven tools to help manage the inherent challenges in those overlaps. We decided their plan of action would be instituting clear values, rules, and laws for the family enterprise, along with adopting different continuity frameworks to prepare the next generation to be responsible employees and owners in the business. Let's get specific.

For two years, I facilitated formal family meetings every quarter. Everyone in Generation 1 (the parents) and 2 (their children) were invited, and no one missed a session. So here, they certainly demonstrated an abundance of commitment to the process. Together we created a set of family-enterprise governance tools they were able to implement:

- A statement of values, mission, and vision

- A code of conduct

- A family employment policy with detailed criteria for working in the business, along with a family compensation policy

- A leadership development plan for next-generation family members

- A formal organizational structure with job profiles for each role within it

- A family council with representatives from each branch of the family and each generation

- A board of directors

They also engaged a lawyer well-versed in familyenterprise dynamics to prepare a revised shareholders agreement, creating the terms for Generation 2 to eventually become owners of the business. And finally, the owners considered whether to invite a non-family member to join their Board to offer independent, objective, and industry-specific expertise.

This enterprising family's dedication to continuity planning is exemplary and rare. They didn't wait until a crisis forced them into (re)action, and are now set up for long-term success because they engaged in an inclusive, transparent, and fair process. Spending time together to develop healthy governance for the whole system created a deep sense of "familiness"[24]—the unique bundle of resources an enterprise has because of the interaction of the family, its individual members, and the business. No family is without its challenges, but they can be managed with more care and compassion when the container of governance has been built together.

HOME
WORK

Answer this question: How do you govern responsibly?

Since governance is all about accountability, be discerning about which decisions you're making as a leader at home and at work. Which ones are clearly defined, communicated, and accepted? Which ones are confusing, assumed, or challenged by others?

Here's a great tool—adapted by many organizational development consultants—to help you define and manage accountability for small to complex projects. It will align your team/family members, reduce ego trips and power plays, increase focus, and get the best results. When the roles and responsibilities are clearly articulated, decision-making is more streamlined, efficient, and effective. My favorite version is called the *DARCI Accountability Grid:*[25]

Project	Decider/ Delegator Holds the ultimate power re: the project	Accountable Person fully accountable for making the project happen	Responsible Those responsible for doing the work on the project	Consulted Those from whom input will be solicited	Informed Those to be kept apprised of relevant developments
STEP 1					
STEP 2					
STEP 3					
STEP 4					

You can use this tool to design a new product launch, organize a family reunion, develop your strategic planning process, or do a kitchen reno! It is also an excellent teaching tool for kids to take ownership of their roles— to offer them more participation, and eventually more power in family decision-making.

CHANGE

Manage
Uncertainty without
Losing Your Center

THE MYSTERY OF THE

MAYBE-NESS OF IT ALL.

SIRI AGRELL

ONE OF THE lessons a leader in a constantly changing system learns is how to stay resilient despite always being pushed off their center. When you're in charge, everyone wants something from you. People gravitate to the leader for all kinds of things—to be fed, to receive advice or love or feedback, to complain, to ask for a raise or a promotion or more toys or a later curfew or just attention. The list goes on . . . forever.

There used to be these children's plastic blow-up mannequins with sand in the bottom that would go down with a punch and pop back up to squeals of delight. Well, that's you. Resilient leaders have a strong enough core to fend off the constant taps (requests and demands) of their family and team members. Yes, you still go down, but if you're resilient and have created healthy personal and professional boundaries, you fall less often and rebound much faster.

Leaders need presence—that steady, stable, and patient quality—because managing constant change is hard. Radical transformation doesn't happen easily or overnight, and honestly, almost all of the real change I witness happens through the courageous and consistent gathering of incremental steps over time... much more rituals of transformation than sudden revelations from on high.

We have a natural resistance to abandoning the familiar and accepting ambiguity, so we become entrenched in behavioral patterns and relationships even if they're not healthy or functional. Shifting our thoughts, feelings, and actions requires an understanding of the dimensions of change, an ability to navigate through resistance and uncertainty, and a genuine commitment to persevere despite the discomfort.

Families, businesses, and family enterprises endure and succeed because they don't just respond and adapt to the changes coming at them, they also initiate and create change in *anticipation* of what they expect might happen. Leaders know how to preserve the best of their past practices and envision a healthy future state. Consequently, they need to become expert change agents (well, "expert" may be pushing it, but not hiding in a corner denying that change is happening would be a good place to start!).

Change unfolds in natural time, not on a fixed schedule. Managing change, therefore, is a process—it's nonlinear and individual and it is specific to the rhythms of the system and the members within it. I usually see four reaction styles show up in family and team members when change occurs: *Resisters*, *Bystanders* (I call these the "fence-sitters"), *Helpers*, and *Champions*. And because of these different reactions, leaders must understand that people will only go through change at the rate that they can personally make sense of it and internalize it. This process can be chaotic, confusing, and uncertain, and also curious, exciting, and exhilarating. It's a time where everyone in the system must call upon their internal and external resources—like resilience and courage—to inhabit a new state of being and work with some semblance of grace.

The driving force behind every change is the explicit acknowledgment that the status quo will no longer do. The remedy is the action that must be taken to successfully liberate the individual, family, or company from its present state in order to arrive at its desired one. But this recognition does not make what needs to be done simple or easy.

Navigating change begins with understanding what kind of response is right for the change you want or need to make. The tendency is often to immediately throw out the project a team has been working on, or end a relationship, or quit a job, and start all over. And although these drastic measures might be the right ones, they are usually too much, too fast. I ask clients to examine the change through two different lenses or dimensions.

Start with *timing*. Is it anticipatory, a change made in the absence of any imminent threat in the system? Or is it reactive, a change made in response to a crisis, threat, or a once-in-a-lifetime promise that requires immediate action?

Then determine the *scope* of the change to be managed. Is it incremental—an orderly flow or process, each step building upon the previous one? Or is it radical—driven by fundamental shifts, both internal or external, in the system?

Based on these dimensions, your response to the change will vary in intensity and complexity. Perfectionist, anxious

The driving force behind every change is the explicit acknowledgment **that the status quo will no longer do.**

executives, parents, and partners who react to every change as a potential catastrophe or personal affront to their leadership abilities will find this range of response a relief.

Here are four levels of intensity and complexity to choose from, in order of magnitude:

1 **Fine-tune:** Anticipate a change in conditions and take some fairly incremental action to make the most of it.

2 **Adapt:** Respond to a changed environment but stay within your basic game plan. (Here it is important to note that this is reactive; you perceive the change as something happening *to* you.)

3 **Redirect:** Respond to what you anticipate will be a radical shift in your family dynamic or work conditions. (Examples here might be a divorce or a merger.)

4 **Overhaul:** Implement radical change in every aspect of the system, initiated under crisis conditions in reaction to an immediate threat.

CHANGE CASE STUDY: FAMILY BUSINESS

AJ, the founder and controlling owner of a midsize family firm, found he was spending more and more time away from his business than at any time since its opening. An entrepreneur who started with grit (and not much else), AJ built a construction business over three decades and turned it into a success. Life was full with family, work, and travel.

Then his cherished wife died after a long illness, and the raw edge of loss turned his grief into silent privation.

He buried himself in work, growing ever more isolated and depressed. After much encouragement from his three worried adult children, AJ began dating and met a woman of many hobbies and interests. The wells of pleasure and new love grew deep and his focus changed. As he retreated from obsessing about the business, AJ created more space for his kids working in the firm, with the goal of them taking more active roles in leading it.

But the transition was not smooth. Rather, it took on a haphazard and confusing stutter-step route that sometimes led to sibling conflict. After analyzing the timing and scope of the change, we decided that an appropriate response was somewhere between "adapt" and "redirect." The family did not see the father's new love life as a radical change, but they clearly needed a more formal and systematic redirection of business roles and responsibilities.

From the start, the elephant in the room was AJ's retirement. Even though the family needed to have this conversation, they avoided it for years, fearing sibling rivalry, or upsetting their dad by even *suggesting* that he consider retiring. Work used to be his only reason for getting out of bed every morning since their mom died. But the recent change in AJ's life forced them to adapt what they were doing and deal with future succession issues.

I helped steward the development of a formal multi-step and multi-year succession planning process, aimed at determining the rising generation's ownership requirements, roles, and responsibilities for when the owner was retirement-ready. AJ revised his estate plans and worked with advisors to develop a transfer-of-ownership process.

The future leaders were each given clear accountabilities in the business operations once held by AJ, who now became their in-house business coach. And they started leadership development programs to work on their emotional intelligence skills, which they realized were much more difficult than the technical ones!

Engaging all members of this family was critical to successfully implementing the transfer of leadership to the next generation and regaining harmony in their relationships. They understood that the system had to retain its wholeness. Without all the members involved, the equilibrium would be disrupted and the interdependence of their relationships lost. Without ongoing engagement there can be no commitment. And that's a dealbreaker, because commitment is the force that moves people through change.

The family moved through 4 stages of commitment:[26]

1 **Awareness:** This is when they realized the change was in fact imminent and understood that the past way of doing something was really over. *Dad was letting go and the next generation family members were moving up.*

2 **Acceptance:** Once the family understood the nature and intent of the change, and were clear on the timing and the scope, they were ready to accept it. *They were adapting to the change in their roles incrementally: for Dad, from leader to coach, and for the children, from workers to successors.*

3 **Adoption:** They became adopters when everyone took on the tangible work of change for which they were

each accountable. *They worked with advisors to plan the transfer of ownership, and they committed to ongoing leadership development and training.*

4 **Advocacy:** As AJ created more space for the rising generation to lead, they expanded their business acumen and confidence, and everyone began to articulate a personal ownership of the change to the outside world. *They had become advocates.*

CHANGE: THE CROSSOVER

Change leadership requires a growth mindset. But leaders cannot discount the resistance (be it hostile, insidious, or neutral by virtue of neglect and inaction) they will face and the force of change they encounter. A system will always return to homeostasis, a steady state of being, even if it's not the ideal shape or sentiment. Barriers to accepting change can include a perceived lack of need, a negative family or organizational climate, a fear of learning, or a history of poorly managed change. If the change is contrary to the self-interest of a team or violates the ideals, values, or norms of the family, the resistance will override the effort.

And then there are the barriers to actioning the change: lacking the support, skills, and resources, poor timing, or no perceived reward for the change. Recognizing the conditions for failure is just as important a leadership skill as identifying those for success. For instance, don't move to make a change when the organization is contracted in crisis; don't assume your staff are *able* to institute the change when they are only just willing; don't think a Board Chair—who feigns support but is making their doubts clear behind the scenes—will become the advocate you need her to be.

Here is the story of a leader who could have quickly fallen into what I call "resistance traps," but didn't. She tempered her drive for change with reason. She knew that gaining the commitment of her staff to a new way of doing things was essential, and went into this project with a highly collaborative mindset.

CHANGE CASE STUDY: WORK

Introducing a new performance management process into an organization is always a challenge. As soon as you start talking about someone's performance at work, it's an immediate trigger for every past and present insecurity, failing, disappointment, and unresolved feeling of perceived betrayal by once-admired bosses. That's just a partial list of what can flash through the mind of someone receiving any kind of feedback on how they're doing at their job. Basically, it's a minefield.

KC, the CEO of a small tech company, knew this, and decided to introduce a first-time formal performance feedback process. The scope of this change was more of a redirection than an adaptation, because the majority of the staff had never received any kind of proper or meaningful review in their past jobs. Compassionate to this, KC wanted the change to be a welcome, positive initiative to increase employee engagement and organizational effectiveness. She'd been around the block on this one, and was going to avoid the classic worrying, avoiding, and resisting that can happen with any change initiative.

Right from the top, the framing was completely different from the usual top-down I'm-in-charge-you're-not appraisal process. This would be a collaborative and continuous conversation between employees and their managers aimed at setting mutually agreed goals, developing skills, checking on progress, and supporting success.

Clear communication is paramount. Whenever a change is announced, people have questions and concerns. In anticipation of possible resistance, we used the 5 Ps of Change checklist to find our footing, prepare answers, and offer our rationale for instituting the new performance feedback tool.[27]

1   **Purpose:** First we explained the purpose of the new process, why we were doing it, and what we were trying to accomplish. We knew that if the staff had a clear sense of purpose, they would be more likely to accept the change.

2   **Picture:** We co-created the big picture by describing our desired outcome, how it would work, and how it would feel for each person. If you give people a picture of what you're trying to create, with a clear destination, they will keep going with you.

3   **Plan:** We laid out the plan of how we were going to develop the process and implement the tool (with details, diagrams, and dates!), because the destination alone isn't enough. If you don't offer a step-by-step *path* that leads people to the desired outcome, you will lose their confidence.

4 **Part**: We allocated the part each person would play in the initiative. The most common question asked in any change initiative is: "What's in it for me?" In response, we gave everyone a role to engage them and increase their commitment from awareness to advocacy.

5 **Patience:** We allotted time for the change to be accepted and adopted. In this initiative, we patiently worked the kinks out of the process. We supported the managers in their skill-building through training and follow-up coaching on giving clear and effective performance feedback to staff.

The phased-in process began with a conversation between managers and direct reports, collaboratively creating goals for the next year and some action plans to achieve them. At the end of the first year, everyone was asked to reflect on their own performance, and the managers convened another conversation to discuss the results. We made slight changes to improve the language, and by the end of Year 1 most staff had become full adopters of the new process.

By sharing this rationale for change, and taking deliberate action one step at a time, KC was able to tame much of the resistance and heighten the team's level of commitment. Once we knew that most staff were not only aware but also accepting of this change, we developed the process with ongoing consultation, review, revision, and approval over the next few years until it became part of the company's talent management culture.

Answer this question: How do you lead through uncertainty and not lose your courage and compassion?

1 Identify a change that you would like to initiate at home or at work.
   - Is the timing anticipatory or reactive?
   - Is the scope of the change incremental or radical?

2 Determine your best response: fine-tune, adapt, redirect, or overhaul?

3 Find answers to the 5 Ps for your specific situation.

Remember, the best way to minimize people's resistance and boost their commitment to change is to provide a balanced approach to communication by responding to their need for information and engagement:

1 **Purpose:** Why is this change being introduced, and why now?

2 **Big Picture:** What is the longer-term vision?

3 **Plan:** What are the timelines and measures of success that will mark progress toward achieving the change?

4   **Parts to Be Played:** What are the interdependencies among different people that will contribute to the achievement of success?

5   **Patience:** What can you do to support your family and team members to accept, adopt, and even advocate for this change at the rate they can personally internalize it?

RELATIONSHIPS

Nurture and Inspire the Best in Everyone

TO LOVE WELL IS THE
TASK IN ALL MEANINGFUL
RELATIONSHIPS, NOT JUST
ROMANTIC BONDS.

BELL HOOKS

THE BEST LEADERS I have known engender a sense of fidelity. I don't mean a wielding of authority to force reverence, allegiance, or obedience—this isn't power-tripping from some kind of malicious intent. Rather, these leaders provoke loyalty and even love because they just know how to connect with an open heart. Everyone in their orbit feels like they matter, and that their ideas and efforts count. Even if the leader is working hard under the surface to make that magic connection happen (sorting through the emotional cues, reading and responding to body language, mirroring words and tone), it comes across as a natural expression of caring for and being interested in others. Of course, leaders—be they presidents or parents—are infallibly human like the rest of us, but the good ones have an exquisite relational intelligence that truly inspires.

There is a perception out there that the skills leaders use to develop meaningful, effective, and nourishing relationships are "soft." It's curious to me how this timeworn characterization of technical or "hard" skills is considered more valuable in the hierarchy of leadership competency. It is much more difficult to create healthy relationships than any subject matter expertise that excludes the human-to-human dynamic. Relational leaders possess self-awareness and sensitivity. They recognize their own motivations, acknowledge and manage their emotions, show empathy and compassion for others' experience, and adapt their communication to create meaningful connections.

Certainly, families are more intimate systems than workplaces, and the degree to which these skills are honed is different. But there is a symmetry in the significance of rousing others to grow, learn, and experiment in safety, to offer undivided attention, positive reinforcement, recognition, truth-telling, and even tough love. A parent's job is to give their kids the unconditional love and support, stimulation, and skills (both hard and soft) to develop into healthy and happy adults. A manager's role is to act as a mentor of effort and excellence, to remove the roadblocks that hinder their employees' performance so they may achieve their goals, and to reward them for a job well done. Both of these roles nurture their relationships by inspiring the people around them to become their very best selves.

So, what does a nurturing leader look like? What is the organizational framework through which these leaders can use their exceptional relational skills to be encouraging coaches and mentors? Here's a story about a tech company's brain drain and the process they took to plug it by nurturing the talent they already had.

Leaders inspire the people around them to become their very best selves.

RELATIONSHIPS CASE STUDY: WORK

The firm was losing a lot of high performers, and it was becoming increasingly difficult to make excuses for the ongoing exodus. After a few years in the position they were hired into, the most motivated, passionate, and creative employees wanted a chance to grow and develop in their careers through lateral moves and promotions. As in almost all industries now, the days of a 25-year career in the same place and leaving with a gold watch were long over. The average stint in any job was 2–5 years when there was no path for advancement, but the firm seemed to keep making *external* hires every time there was an opening. This made the existing staff feel unappreciated and, as a consequence, disengaged. Essentially, the leadership was unintentionally creating a "flight-risk talent pool" instead of becoming an "employer of choice."

Their competition, however, was onto them and had headhunters raiding their technical ranks on a regular basis. They were offering HIPOs (high-potential employees) similar compensation but more advancement opportunities and professional development, health and wellness benefits, and sometimes even an executive coach.

All this is to say, the firm was great at attracting the best talent but they were lousy at retaining it.

Another hurdle was the executives' resistance to *sharing* talent. Every department wanted to own their potential leaders, and had created silos of technical excellence. That meant that all the subject-matter expertise was hoarded within, and there was very little transfer of knowledge across the organization. Even if someone from one area was qualified (and interested) in moving to another at a higher level, it would be perceived as a betrayal by their existing department—if they even heard about the opening to begin with.

Finally, the firm's senior leaders were starting to age out of their roles. The risk of losing great people with the skills and experiences—notwithstanding their institutional memory (for instance, of the genesis and evolution of their corporate culture, their key decisions and strategies, the historical relationships that led to certain successes and failures)—was too high to not advance a formal leadership development process. It was time for deliberate investment in and nurturance of young talent.

Working with the Senior Leadership Team (SLT), we built a company-specific Leadership Talent Matrix. It was designed around four dimensions:

- **Competencies:** the observable skills and behaviors leaders can aspire to possess.

- **Experiences:** the roles and/or projects leaders can take on to prepare for a future opportunity.

- **Qualities:** the personality traits or attributes leaders can inhabit and exhibit.

- **Drivers:** the values that can influence leaders' motivation and engagement.

I facilitated multiple SLT conversations to determine what should populate each quadrant. We didn't want to fill the boxes with some vague, generic list we pulled from the internet, but rather a tailored, unique description that combined a) what the present leadership actually looked like, and b) what it aspired to be in the best possible future. When we landed on an acceptable draft, we then shared the Matrix with the next level of management to hear their feedback and test its accuracy and usability. More conversations later, we settled on a Matrix that everyone could support and put into action. It looked like this:

LEADERSHIP TALENT MATRIX	
Competencies	**Experiences**
Business/financial acumen	Led large-scale change initiatives
Organizational "savvy"	Managed risks and crises
Team leadership	Resolved conflicts
Stakeholder relations	Managed all aspects of a business
Systems thinking	
Effective decision-making	
Traits	**Drivers**
Resilience	Commitment to people, planet, and profit
Emotional intelligence	Making an impact
Collaboration	Getting results
Communication	Equity, diversity, and inclusion
Bravery	Being of service

This Talent Matrix served many aims: It established a formal organizational development and training process, and gave leaders an essential coaching framework to develop and engage their staff. It defined how leaders could show up as inspiring role models, demonstrating the defined talents in real time . . . walking the walk as well as talking the talk. And it allowed for more meaningful and focused conversations, nourishing the one-on-one relationships between leaders and direct reports to create deeper bonds of trust and connection. When you think about it, most people spend more time with their workmates than they do with their family members, so these relationships have to matter. And it's incumbent upon the leader to initiate those relationships and create the conditions of reciprocity, resonance, and respect.

RELATIONSHIPS: THE CROSSOVER

But sometimes these work relationships overshadow the ones at home. Over the years I have worked with many women leaders who are so over-functioning professionally that there's nothing left for their non-work lives. Nurturing *themselves* isn't even an afterthought. Typically these kinds of leaders arrive in my office in various stages of psychological distress—exhaustion, depression, confusion, and resentment. And since gender roles often play a big part here, there's one more form of distress to acknowledge: guilt. This particular yet common emotion drags and derails even the most resilient client. It's as if the entire history of civilization's expectations of women and mothers has taken residence inside their mind-bodies to become a repeating sequence of their DNA. Most of the time, they have no reason to feel interminably guilty, for they haven't acted to purposefully undermine or damage anyone. They just feel that whatever they're doing, it's never enough. I guess that sometimes men feel this way, but they're not really talking to me about it.

This is a story of a leader who spent decades climbing an elusive ladder of success and felt forced to compartmentalize her work and home selves until she felt pulled apart.

RELATIONSHIP CASE STUDY: HOME AND WORK

GG, the CEO of a media company, began her leadership journey at a time when ambitious women were required to fight against the negative female stereotypes that created barriers to success, power, and influence by behaving like men. The theatre of the boardroom was, and to some extent still is in many sectors, a show of rational force, hierarchical dominance, pragmatism, and competition. GG's "soft" leadership style—compassion, the ability to nurture others, and building meaningful relationships—kept her bumping up against that glass ceiling. So gradually she turned herself into the culturally acceptable kind of leader that the male-led company expected. GG's performance reviews described her as smart, aggressive, cool under pressure, results-focused, and above all, driven to succeed, resulting in a series of promotions until she finally did break that ceiling.

But there were consequences. The demand to become so much a part of that organizational system led to a kind of separation from GG's essential (and true) feminine self. With every advancement received in the corporate ranks, these so-called winning behaviors at work began to bleed into her home life. She gradually became less affectionate and available, showing up more and more in her "boss" clothes, treating her spouse and kids like staff, throwing out orders and constantly trying to exert control. Although there were many red flags flying over that time and even more excuses made ("Mom's just tired—she's under a lot of pressure"), things continued to get worse. When the family finally reacted against her emotional distance and insisted on more love and kindness from GG, it drove her further into panic mode.

When we are under extreme stress our mind-bodies react in powerful ways: We notice those cues around us that make us feel unsafe. Our brain begins to process those cues and shifts our physiological state from welcoming and comfortable to one of danger. To adapt to this threat, we can respond in three ways: *freeze, flee,* or *fight.* GG did all three and it showed up in her behaviors. Instead of softening to the entreaties of her family, she became more combative. She was losing her discernment and making bad decisions in both the work and the home fronts, tightening her grip on control, becoming impatient and increasingly demanding. Her chaotic and exhausted emotional landscape made her want to run and hide. She felt like a failure and tremendously guilty for causing so much pain for her family and her team. There were warning signs, but GG felt frozen and unable to act, until both her husband and her Board Chair told her to get some help before the cracks became too deep.

My role as GG's therapist was to offer her a safe place to put the pieces back together. I supported her to reflect and relax enough to examine her life and integrate *all* her qualities into a full and whole self—those that contributed to her professional success and family harmony, and those she felt forced to repress in the climb. In the beginning GG was reticent and well-defended, but slowly she opened to her raw and real feelings. I was a witness to the courageous conversations she was having with herself so that she could, through curiosity and self-compassion, understand what happened and why, and to figure out where to go next.

GG realized that this split in her thoughts and behavior negatively affected her family, her employees, and ultimately her own mental health and resilience. Chasing the chimera of power and all the privileges that came with it had forced her to toughen. But the costs were too great and the rewards too empty. Why did she need to hold onto those regressive masculine-traited definitions of leadership? How could she reconnect with her powerful feminine qualities and bring those into the boardroom? In her search to redefine leadership, GG struggled to create a new narrative of how she could show up authentically, and ultimately be a whole leader to her team.

GG deeply grieved the damage this hardening had done to her family relationships. Although she didn't mean to abandon her role as a nurturing mother and spouse, she still felt guilty for not having the strength to fight the powerful and insidious messages she received in the workplace. How could she forgive herself for hurting people she loved and cared for, even if it wasn't intentional? How could this new narrative support her to be a loving family member?

After enough time spent in reflection, GG moved into action. She identified what would be the most desired outcomes for herself, her family members, her team, and her renewed relationships with all of them. She started having more authentic and vulnerable conversations with her spouse, kids, and team members. She took responsibility for her behavior and put her nurturance "muscle" into high gear. She began a mindfulness practice to support her *presence* in her relationships, started asking her family "What can I do for you?" instead of making demands on them, and became a less controlling, more collaborative, and compassionate partner in the workplace. She was able to show up in a very different way. GG's family and staff experienced her as steadier and more sensitive to their needs and desires. They saw her as an active listener, an inspiring leader, and a more loving parent and partner.

GG, and many clients like her, taught me that sometimes we need to crash (or crumble) before committing to an examined life. This journey of self-discovery, although difficult and demanding, presents leaders with the opportunity to study their motivations, and clarify what matters most. Additionally, it offers them the freedom to make the changes each require for a more resilient and fulfilling life.

Answer this question: How can you help others become their best selves?

Here are a few guidelines to nurture your relationships with kindness and respect:

Ask, don't assume: Start with communicating in a way that attends to the specific needs of your listener. Ask these questions:

> In order for me to communicate with you as effectively as possible, what should I do?

> What should I avoid doing?

> What kind of information do you want to receive from me first?

I once walked into a meeting with M, a senior executive client who I knew had no time to waste (or rather, I *assumed* had no time to waste). Thinking I was being respectful, I sat down, opened my file, pulled out my notes, and immediately addressed the first item on our agenda. After a few minutes, M stopped me and said, "What are you doing? I can't just start talking business with you. I need to warm up with some small talk!" I'll always be grateful to M for the reminder that it's up to me to ask my interlocutor what kind of communication they want from me, not make assumptions about what *I* think they need. The lesson for leaders, then, is that you can't get to inspiration until you create an effective communication language with a follower so they can really hear you. Asking these questions makes them feel like they really matter.

Treat every encounter as your last: Not to be maudlin, but there are no guarantees you will have infinite opportunities to be with a family or team member... or to even have one more conversation, meeting, or visit after your last. A mentor once reminded me that "every relationship is a series of hellos and goodbyes," so make each one count. One of the best ways to inspire someone is to make them feel that their presence has elevated and inspired you to be the best leader, parent, partner, friend, or colleague. Show your gratitude by giving each person your undivided attention. It will inspire their best efforts in return.

Go deep: Be real and show up as your whole and authentic self. Admit when you're wrong, and encourage others to learn from their mistakes as you have. Being vulnerable builds trust, which is the oxygen of true relationships. When you go deep (versus staying on the surface) you will invite others to get to know the real you, and they will hopefully reciprocate with their true experiences and aspirations.

Don't micromanage: Nobody likes a control freak. Give people the tools, information, and personal agency to work on a project, learn a new skill, or create healthy habits. Then be there to nurture their progress, offer feedback, and celebrate and cherish their efforts so they can move consistently toward successful outcomes and nourished lives. Everyone needs a cheerleader. No one needs a micromanager.

LEGACY

Foster Continuity and a Well-Planned Succession

IF YOUR ACTIONS CREATE
A LEGACY THAT INSPIRES
OTHERS TO DREAM MORE,
LEARN MORE, DO MORE, AND
BECOME MORE, THEN YOU ARE
AN EXCELLENT LEADER.

DOLLY PARTON

EVERYONE WANTS TO feel like they matter. They want their relationships, their work, and their lives to matter. And one of the useful ways of thinking about "how things matter" is through their impact: "What did I do, and what did it all mean?"

As you've seen through these past lessons, leadership requires a vigilance on many fronts, but perhaps none so existential as leaving a mark. These questions can progress from "What am I doing with my career?" to "Am I leaving things better than I found them?" and all the way through "Have I developed people who can carry on the best of my work and build on the values I have tried to embody?" Another way of asking this question: "What is my legacy?"

Good leaders perform well in the here and now, but great leaders see further. They steward their families, their businesses, and everything they touch toward a strong future—ensuring the continuity of each of these systems through time and even generations. Is there a recipe for this stewardship? Can we translate it into a deliberate, formal, and repeatable process?

In this final lesson, we're going to concentrate exclusively on one domain: the family enterprise. Because in these systems, there is almost always a desire to build a legacy from one generation to the next. But desire is not enough. There must be a committed and intentional focus on leadership succession. This really is "where the rubber meets the road."

There are many rewards for developing a formal succession plan for future leaders. It enhances the value of the organization by retaining the most talented successors. It offers a fresh outlook on safe—even staid—strategies and a transformative angle on doing things differently. It can create clarity for everyone by lessening anxiety about who will assume leadership, and most importantly, it fosters a legacy for the business. And through the succession process, we give those gifted with leadership potential the opportunity to make a difference, stretch their limits, and strive to new heights. Succession planning is a time-consuming and strenuous exercise, but it is critical to the firm's overall performance and enduring prosperity.

Yet many leaders don't prepare anyone to succeed them. Why not? Well, mostly because they don't believe anyone can. A second obstacle is that for those leadership teams who try to implement a succession plan, they often disagree on what "potential" is and who has it. A final stumbling block occurs if a successor is named—but then left high and dry without proper preparation, critical information, or the tools to do the job effectively.

Happily, there are those future-oriented leaders who do invest the discipline, money, and time. This results in a strong bench of possible successors who are driven to better themselves, engage their teams, and advance their organizations. And there's another remarkable secondary benefit I've witnessed: it is beautiful to see how the relationships between dedicated mentors and their devoted successors grow... the sharing of life experiences, the mutual learning, and the strengthening of personal bonds that can last a lifetime.

For family business leaders—often deeply invested in their overlapping home and work lives—nurturing talented successors to foster a family legacy presents a more complex and often precarious path. Simply put, it is close to impossible to remain objective when considering a relative's future capacity to assume one's own leadership role.

Let's look at an example. W runs his business like a family: Everyone on staff is treated like one of his kids; he knows the names of their children; he tells them when they need a break and to take a vacation. He even plays the matchmaker with some of the single employees. He is confident in his leadership, believing himself to be warm, involved, approachable, and caring.

His successor-niece, J, has a very different management style. W believes that the staff perceives J as cold, hasty in her decision-making, and detached from the day-to-day. When the uncle gives her feedback to "soften her style a bit," J gets defensive. (She in turn finds W's management style to be indulgent, micromanaging, and crippled with unhealthy boundaries between management and staff.)

Good leaders perform well in the here and now, but **great leaders see further.**

They argue, and then they both shut down. It ends in a mess. Neither can be objective about themself or each other. Can there be *any* objectivity when it comes to family business?

First, planning is critical. Succession will almost always fail if there isn't dedicated preparation. But what does that preparation look like?

It looks hard. All of the elements need to progress simultaneously, so let's break them out: The business needs to be prepared as a self-sustaining entity with clear strategies, goals, and controls. As discussed in the previous lesson, the successors need their talent developed in accordance with the values, skills, and knowledge required for leadership. The family needs to be prepared to not just accept the successor(s) but to support them—no undermining, no dissension. The ownership team needs to be prepared to deal with more than one successor, as it is now more common for founding owners to pass the baton to sibling partnerships or even cousin consortiums. All of these require lots of practice, learning about effective teamwork, shared decision-making, and resolving those inevitable conflicts.

But here is where things get real and the effectiveness of the plan gets tested: preparing for the current leader to transition *out* of the business. If this isn't done well—with structures and facilitation that ensures extraordinary amounts of respect, patience, discipline, and loving compassion—then the whole succession adventure can descend into chaos. It is not uncommon for those leaders to fight or fear relinquishing control. The word "loving" here is important because almost always the devotion and affection in the family are forgotten in the heightened emotion of this part of the process. I often need to remind them, "Remember that you said how much you love the kids and how proud you are of their business savvy?" Or, "You know how difficult this can be on your dad, so how about a bit more love and a little less judgment?"

Here's a story about three brothers, who together owned and ran a successful family business, but who also knew that they were getting older and needed to transition to new leadership. They wanted to help steward the next family chapter of the business, but they were also concerned with both their individual and collective legacies. These are like-minded players with pretty clear objectives, so this is going to be pretty straightforward, right? Well, not so fast.

LEGACY CASE STUDY: FAMILY BUSINESS

Three brothers—P, S, and Y—were born and raised on their parents' dairy farm and are still there . . . meeting for their morning coffee ritual, in the office, every day, for the last fifty years. The farm is much bigger now than when they went to work there full-time after high school. Over the decades, they worked hand-in-hand with their parents to acquire more land, grow more capital, and take on some smart risks to expand their business. When I met them, the operation included the original farm, a food production arm, and a land development company. When their parents passed away, each son received an equal share of all the family assets. And the sibling partnership in this second generation has been surprisingly steady and strong since they took on full ownership control. P, S, and Y told me, "We aren't just brothers, we're best friends," and it showed. Their shared family values of responsibility, respect, and gratitude have guided them well. The enterprise was solid and all three families were financially secure.

Their commitment to creating a family legacy was obvious in how they've incorporated their next generation into the business. P, S, and Y learned on the job, but decided that their children should have more formal training—even gaining some years of work experience *away* from the farm so that they could bring in new ideas from the outside world. The brothers helped pay for post-secondary education for those who wanted it. One of the tendencies in family enterprises is to keep the rising generation's roles and responsibilities informal (no job titles and no formal job descriptions, for example). But here they created formal titles and genuine decision-making authority...to a point.

The "kids"—the third generation—were themselves now in their fifties and were *really* ready to take over. The brothers knew it was time. Still, they just couldn't let go. Relinquishing their leadership and control of the business was terrifying, since every aspect of their individual and collective lives was inextricably tied to the family business. It defined them. Who were they if not its leaders?

When P, S, and Y tried to imagine letting go, their resistance-rationalizations became conversation stoppers: "Retirement would be the death of us." "The business will fall apart without us." "The kids won't need us anymore."

And my favorite, "Our wives won't want us around all the time." The most common anxiety of all, however, really struck at the heart of what we mean when we talk about legacy: "Who will I *be* if I leave?"

The fear and insecurity they felt were all-consuming. The brothers felt sure that they had done so many of the right things to create capable successors. And those successors were itching to fully step into their leadership shoes. But while all the technical (head) structures and processes were in place for the third generation's succession, the owners' hearts were stuck, undermining the entire process. They "promised to leave" but were unable to fully relinquish control. And as you can imagine, the kids (remember, they were men and women in their fifties, but I'm reflecting the language their fathers used) were becoming restless and resentful. The conversation with their dads around transferring ownership had been going on for five years—a revolving door of P, S, and Y leaving without proper planning, and then reappearing to take back decision-making—each time reversing any changes their kids had made in their absence. It was time for an intervention.

LEGACY: APPROACH

Managing a transition is different from bringing about a change. I learned this simple but illuminating truth years ago from William Bridges, the guru of transition management. His work helped me understand how textured and complex a process it can be for people to move on successfully from whatever state they were in to the next one.[28]

Essentially, people need to do three things:

- Let go of the old identities.

- Journey through a process to internalize the transition.

- Create a new beginning.

I've used this theory and methodology with many clients who are transitioning out of relationships or careers and making other life changes.

Bridges makes a clear distinction between change and transition. Change is an event. Something stops and it is external in nature. In this case, the retirement party happens, the new ownership papers are signed, the letterhead is different. But in the case of P, S, and Y's *transition* into retirement—where something ends and something new begins—it is an *internal process*, a gradual psychological, emotional, and spiritual reorientation that happens inside each brother as they try to adapt to the change. This is about their loss of identify and their whole world. With change, the shift starts in the head and can be quick. But with transition, it starts in the heart. Transition requires dedicated time for a healthy adjustment and full acceptance.

My work started with the retirement-reluctant co-owners. I congratulated them on being proactive (better late than never!) rather than passing on their business "cold turkey"—an all-too-common scenario where the next generation takes charge because a death, illness, or accident forces a sudden departure. I supported each of them to work through their many inner dialogues of resistance, fear, and confusion. It was remarkable how much of this was shared by all three, and just talking about their feelings enabled a collective understanding. There was an *emotional unraveling*—a process to discover how to let go of leadership control without dissolving into nothingness.

Bridges' first phase—*Endings*—is about disengaging from the old ways and letting go of who we were. It's experiencing the loss, finding a sense of closure, and saying goodbye. To get through this phase, P, S, and Y were able to articulate, acknowledge, and honor their losses: their sense of purpose and power as hardworking men who provided for their families; their comfort in having a place to go and people to connect with every day; and their reputation in the community as the guys who "made it." They started to find ways to compensate for some of the losses. Keeping their morning ritual at a coffee shop in their town instead of at the farm office was healing. We created a safe space for them to grieve their losses but not their personal agency. Rituals are excellent regulators of emotions and social connection, so they developed some to help mark endings. They made a touching memory book of their years working together, including mementos, photos, articles, and awards they had collected over the years. They worked with an artist who photographed each piece and designed the book. Then, the brothers carved a box to hold these memories, which sits at the farm office in a place of pride.

A second phase of managing transitions is called the *Neutral Zone*. For the brothers, this meant a confusing in-between time where they weren't exactly sure who they were going to become. It demanded the establishment of a new cadence for the everyday. We brought in their successor sons and daughters to plan for a gradual but deliberate phasing out of the brothers' everyday management roles and responsibilities. Based on their particular subject-matter expertise, the three would become advisors to the rising generation leadership group, as well as individual coaches to each leader, throughout the next year. These new roles were a value-add to the business, allowing the brothers to stay meaningfully connected. But mostly, it helped get them through the wilderness period of transition.

In my individual conversations with P, S, and Y, I asked them to be curious: What were they interested in? How did they want to fill their days? Y wanted to learn how to play golf, P signed up for a cycling group, and S had care of his grandchildren a few mornings a week. Gradually they all became more involved in their community as active volunteers, joining boards as proud representatives of their family. As time passed, they realized how much they all enjoyed this new contribution of time and energy.

The need to "contribute" is powerful. And it facilitates a natural progression to the third phase of managing transition: *New Beginnings*—a re-energizing period of growing familiar with and accepting the new reality. Beginnings are actually the easiest part of any transition if you have crafted a proper ending and managed the neutral zone well. And P,S, and Y did a great job of it, defining their successful retirement as a chance to create a second career with a renewed purpose. Faithful to their family values of responsibility, respect, and gratitude, they created a family foundation to give back to their community, becoming enthusiastic students of family philanthropy. The brothers successfully translated their commitment to continuity into building a legacy of giving from one generation to the next.

The change of leadership is just the tip of the iceberg. The transition for those letting go of one role and finding meaning in another requires patience, self-compassion, and courageous self-awareness. This is the human side of family-enterprise succession. In our conversations, each brother described his own unique process in managing the transition—sometimes clinging intractably to what was known and secure, sometimes experiencing a freedom and excitement for what could be. I helped them manage the rollercoaster. I was there to listen to their stories, to offer structure through proven frameworks and methodologies, to help them make sense of their strong emotions as they transitioned from leading only their business to leading their whole lives. The only way to do that successfully was to help them integrate all their different parts—parents, owners, operators, managers, spouses, siblings, grand-parents, community leaders—into a whole self. Home and work. Together.

HOME
WORK

Answer this question: What does a well-planned transition and leadership continuity look like?

1 Using the Leadership Talent Matrix for your organization as a guide (see Lesson 7), identify your possible successors.

2 Build a succession plan for the high-potential leaders in your organization. Here's a list of development opportunities you can offer your candidates for succession that can apply to family and non-family enterprises.

- Offer candidates cross-training opportunities or temporary assignments in other departments to learn all aspects of your business and the skills required to excel.
- Provide coaching from trusted mentors within the business or from objective external experts.
- Encourage them to participate in both industry and peer support groups in order to expand their networks and increase their knowledge.
- Send them for formal leadership training to build those skills.

- Give them increasing levels of responsibility, such as managing their own P&L, acting as the company representative, becoming a board director, and so on.

3 Develop strategies for yourself to move through the 3 phases of transition:

Endings
- Name, acknowledge, and honor your losses.
- Redefine, reinvent, replace, or relinquish what you've lost.
- Grieve for those losses using rituals or symbols to mark your endings.
- Identify the anchors in your life. Notice what is *not* changing.

Neutral Zone
- This can be a lonely place, so seek out the individuals and groups who know what you're going through for support, information, and resources.
- Make use of temporary solutions and arrangements without having to commit to one plan for good. Try things out.
- This is a time to be creative. Remember, you're in Possibility Land, so enhance your learning and capitalize on the opportunities that come your way.

Beginnings

- Fine-tune your plan for a new role, identity, and purpose.
- Give yourself time and attention to translate these changes into new attitudes and behaviors.
- Be open to making adaptations to your plans; don't freak out and get stuck in absolutes.
- Try for a few quick wins early on to help build your confidence for more.

FINAL THOUGHTS
Constant Accountability

ATTENTION IS THE TRUE

SOURCE OF WEALTH.

SAM HARRIS

EADERSHIP CAN SOMETIMES be exhilarating, exhausting, motivating, chaotic, and even transformational. But it is always hard. The responsibilities of the role are weighty and consequential. As many leaders have shared with me, making difficult decisions—be they complex, controversial, or mundane—is a lonely and isolating experience. Although excellent leaders smartly align themselves with skilled team members, trusted advisors, and loving partners, being in charge is mostly a solitary exercise of constant accountability.

So here, in a final thought, I'd like to offer an inversion of the advice and learnings I've tried to share: In your workplaces and home spaces, you are the one always paying attention to the needs of others. But who's paying attention to *you*?

A persistent reflection (and grievance) from my clients over the years is that seldom are they themselves given enough attention and thought—which is actually why I originally decided to write this book. I wanted to give you *my* full attention by offering a systemic lens to understand and navigate the rich and complex landscapes of your professional and personal leadership lives.

But you're busy, and all the stories and learnings I presented in both parts of the book may appear to you a bit overwhelming. So here are three takeaways, reflections, and reminders on how you can use this information:

1   **Your leadership learning journey is an ongoing process.** Like any professional or personal development, it involves more than a few hurried moments of contemplation wedged in between the ongoing disruptions, preoccupations, and difficulties of the many responsibilities you hold at work and at home. Ideally, you'd be able to create the time and the space to focus on yourself without distraction. But for most leaders, the time to freely examine and experiment is precious, and you just don't have enough of it. So look at your leadership development as a journey and not a destination. This is probably true of many things, but it's especially true here and now.

2   **You don't have to do all of this at once.** Because there are so many tools and techniques to choose from, where do you begin? Here are some "start-with" strategies:

- Which leadership qualities and leadership lessons have the most resonance for you and your present context? Which ones sparked your interest and curiosity? Perhaps you've found yourself asking, "Do my values align with my teams'?" or "Who in my family business would actually have the competencies to succeed me?" or "Is it possible to be compassionate and give someone feedback that could lead to their dismissal?" Reflecting on which leadership lessons made the biggest impression on you while you read about them is a good place to start.

- Which lessons made you nervous—even anxious—because you know something's wrong or missing in your leadership? Another way to think of this is, What engenders a sense of urgency for you? Perhaps you've been thinking something like, "I've been pretending that my partner and I are on the same parenting page . . . but we really aren't." Or, "We've set a totally unrealistic and unclear marketing strategy that we're never going to achieve." Or, "I'm definitely burned out."

- How much time can you reasonably commit to your own learning and development? Some of the tools described in this book are quick to implement and can be easily incorporated into your daily leadership practice (like putting your phone away and just actively listening to your kids, or starting every team meeting with a review of your Code of Conduct). Some take a longer time to practice and integrate (developing your corporate vision, mission, and values, or finding the discipline to create a DARCI for every project) in order for their impact to be felt. Pick and choose from the simplest and quickest, and work your way up.

The bottom line is to decide where you can get the most traction from your efforts, and then to choose the interventions that will make the most sense for your leadership journey.

3   **You're in the relationship business.** Being a leader is all about building authentic and meaningful connections with other people, and fostering healthy, resilient systems—be they at home or at work. The depth and breadth of these connections will, of course, vary, but your "job" is to understand and meet others' needs... constantly. That means you are a guide, mentor, coach, partner, confidante, attendant, teacher, supporter, and advisor all in one. As I wrote in the introduction, "Leading any kind of social system (family or business) is the hardest job in the world." This is a reminder that your resilience to recognize, discern, and manage all your different types of relationships—the complexities, subtleties, and "mind-fields"—needs to be high. Your self-care is essential, because as a leader, if you go down, there's a good chance that everyone else will too. Be accountable to yourself first, so that you can be *successful* at being accountable to others.

My hope is that you will thrive in your leadership, and that the qualities and lessons I've shared will be useful, repeatable, and supportive—wherever you lead. Whether corporate, organizational, or family systems, be you president, partner, or parent—your goal is to show up as your whole, healthy, and integrated self. That is *true* leadership.

ACKNOWLEDGMENTS

F ROM A VERY young age, I have had an intense interest in how people live and work, and have wanted to capture their interior dialogues through the magnifying glass of my focused attention. I've always wanted to understand what happens within and between people; as Susan Sontag wrote, "I am interested in various kinds of passionate engagement." My desire to learn about and then try to understand the heart's yearnings, the mind's complexities, and the delicate dance of a relationship's expanding and contracting nature led me to a career that compels me to listen to other people's stories of work and home.

So, I listen for a living. Listening has been my way of offering complete attention and generosity to my clients. My sincere thanks and gratitude to them—my greatest teachers—for courageously sharing their curiosities, concerns, and complexities with me over the decades.

This book would not have been possible if not for the people who've been so generous with their wisdom and

ATTENTION IS THE

RAREST AND PUREST

FORM OF GENEROSITY.

SIMONE WEIL

support to me throughout my career. Heartfelt appreciation to my supervisors and mentors, all gifted leaders in their fields, who taught me how to listen: Virginia Satir, Maria Gomori, Jay Lappin, Bruce Buchanan, William Bridges, Lorne Plunkett, Jean-Claude Gauthier, and Andrew Feldmar.

Thank you to my own personal (and very patient) board of advisors who got me going, and kept me going on this project: Tzeporah Berman, Janie Brown, Pam Chaloult, Prem Gill, Branislav Henselmann, Robyn Hooper, Priya Huffman, Carrie Saxifrage, and Libby Yager. Thanks to Sadhu Johnstone for his inspiring leadership, and to the glorious team at Page Two Books, especially Jesse Finkelstein and "My Editor" extraordinaire, Amanda Lewis.

Many years ago, my brilliant and talented brother, Allan Chochinov, came up with the far-fetched idea that I should write a book about how the different parts of my work made a whole career. I want to thank him for the countless hours of listening, questioning, teaching, challenging, cheering, and hand-holding he so generously offered to get me to the finish line. I could *never* have done it without him.

And finally, my thanks and gratitude to my husband, Eric Posen, the embodiment of limitless love, who creates the most perfect container in which all my pursuits can grow.

NOTES

1   Alfredo De Massis, Federico Frattini, Antonio Majocchi, and Lucia
    Piscitello, "Family firms in the global economy: Toward a deeper
    understanding of internationalization determinants, processes,
    and outcomes," *Global Strategy Journal* 8, no. 1 (2018): 3-21.

2   Family Enterprise Xchange Foundation, *Family Enterprise Matters:
    Harnessing the Most Powerful Driver of Economic Growth in Canada*
    (Oakville, ON: Family Enterprise Xchange Foundation, 2019),
    familyenterprise.ca/wp-content/uploads/2020/01/FEX-2019
    -Report-Family-Enterprise-Matters.pdf.

3   "Family Business Statistics," *Resources for Entrepreneurs*, gaebler.com
    /Family-Business-Statistics.htm.

4   Daryl R. Conner, *Managing at the Speed of Change: How Resilient
    Managers Succeed and Prosper Where Others Fail* (New York: Random
    House, 1993).

5   "Critical Thinking Cheatsheet," *Future Focused Learning*,
    get.futurefocusedlearning.net/critical-thinking-cheatsheet.

6   Albert Mehrabian and Morton Wiener, "Decoding of Inconsistent
    Communications," *Journal of Personality and Social Psychology* 6, no. 1
    (1967): 109-114. See also Albert Mehrabian and Susan R. Ferris,
    "Inference of Attitudes from Nonverbal Communication in Two
    Channels," *Journal of Consulting Psychology* 31, no. 3 (1967): 248-252.

7   Stephen W. Porges, "The Neurobiology of Feeling Safe,"
    The Neuropsychotherapist 5, no. 10 (October 10, 2017): 12–23,
    thescienceofpsychotherapy.com/wp-content/uploads/2017/10
    /NPTV5I10.pdf.

8   Lorne C. Plunkett and Robert Fournier, *Participative Management:
    Implementing Empowerment* (New York: Wiley, 1991).

9   Jenny Rooney, "With 'Applied Empathy,' Michael Ventura Spotlights
    Empathy as Competitive Advantage in Business," *Forbes*, May 21,
    2018, forbes.com/sites/jenniferrooney/2018/05/21
    /with-applied-empathy-michael-ventura-spotlights-empathy-as
    -competitive-advantage-in-business.

10 Agata Blaszczak-Boxe, "Too Much Emotional Intelligence Is a Bad
    Thing," *Scientific American Mind*, March 1, 2017, scientificamerican.com
    /article/too-much-emotional-intelligence-is-a-bad-thing. See also
    Kim Armstrong, "'I Feel Your Pain': The Neuroscience of Empathy,"
    Observer 31, no. 1 (January 2018), psychologicalscience.org/observer
    /neuroscience-empathy.

11 Kendra Cherry, "What Is the Negativity Bias?" *Verywell Mind*, April
    29, 2020, verywellmind.com/negative-bias-4589618.

12 Tiffany A. Ito, Jeff T. Larsen, N. Kyle Smith, and John T. Cacioppo,
    "Negative Information Weighs More Heavily on the Brain: The
    Negativity Bias in Evaluative Categorizations," *Journal of Personality
    and Social Psychology* 75, no. 4 (1998): 887–900.

13 Daniel Kahneman and Amos Tversky, "Choices, Values, and
    Frames," American Psychologist 39, no. 4 (1984): 341–350.

14 These phrases are adapted from Sharon Salzberg, *Real Love: The Art
    of Mindful Connection* (New York: Flatiron Books, 2017), 19. Loving
    kindness is a meditation technique rooted in ancient Buddhist
    traditions and teachings. It is a practice to cultivate self-love, inner
    peace, understanding, and empathy for others through the repetition
    of certain phrases to express these intentions.

15 Jay Lappin, "Family Therapy: A Structural Approach," in *Paradigms of Clinical Social Work*, ed. Rachelle A. Dorfman (New York: Brunner/Mazel, 1988), 220–252.

16 Ludo Van der Heyden, Christine Blondel, and Randel S. Carlock, "Fair Process: Striving for Justice in Family Business," *Family Business Review* 18, no. 1 (March 1, 2005): 1–21.

17 "Triangulation," in *Family Therapy Glossary*, 4th edition, eds. Ashley L. Landers, Rikki Patton, and Mallica Reynolds (Alexandria, VA: American Association for Marriage and Family Therapy, 2016), 32.

18 This is from the neuroscientific research on polyvagal theory developed by Stephen Porges, as discussed in, for instance, Ashley Abramson, "If There Was Ever a Time to Activate Your Vagus Nerve, It Is Now," *Medium*, April 10, 2020, elemental.medium.com/if-there-was-ever-a-time-to-activate-your-vagus-nerve-it-is-now-2227e8c6885b.

19 This list is adapted from Craig E. Aronoff and John L. Ward, *Family Business Values: How to Assure a Legacy of Continuity and Success* (New York: Palgrave Macmillan, 2011).

20 I'm grateful to Andrew Feldmar for originally giving me this framework during one of my own therapy sessions.

21 George Stalk, Jr., and Henry Foley, "Avoid the Traps That Can Destroy Family Businesses," *Harvard Business Review* 90 (2012): 25–27, hbr.org/2012/01/avoid-the-traps-that-can-destroy-family-businesses.

22 Matt Wesley in collaboration with Angelo J. Robles, "The Power of Family Culture," white paper (Greenwich, CT: Family Office Association, 2015), 7. hvst.com/posts/the-power-of-family-culture-0x5TBd7J.

23 Henry Mintzberg, "Managing the Strategy Development Process: Deliberate vs. Emergent Strategy," *Harvard Business Review Case Study* (December 11, 2019).

24 This term was introduced and developed in Timothy G. Habbershon and Mary L. Williams, "A Resource-Based Framework for Assessing the Strategic Advantages of Family Firms," *Family Business Review* 12, no. 1 (March 1, 1999): 1–25.

25 This tool is available online at stproject.org/resources/tools-for -transformation (© 2015 Robert Gass).

26 These four stages are loosely adapted from Daryl R. Conner and Robert W. Patterson, "Building Commitment to Organizational Change," *Training and Development Journal* 36, no. 4 (April 1982): 18–30.

27 The 4 Ps of Change comes from the methodology in William Bridges, *Managing Transitions: Making the Most of Change*, 4th edition (Boston: Da Capo Press, 2017). I added #5 (Patience) myself because when leaders don't give enough time to accept and adopt the changes, they don't stick.

28 In addition to *Managing Transitions* (see note 27), an important work is William Bridges, *Creating You & Co.: Learn to Think Like the CEO of Your Own Career* (Boston: Da Capo Press, 1998).

David Ellingsen

DEENA CHOCHINOV is a therapist, management consultant, and family enterprise advisor. She supports executives and senior teams in the corporate and nonprofit sectors, with a focus on leadership coaching, talent management, and organizational development. She advises multigenerational business families who seek the tools and techniques to make smart decisions, manage conflict effectively, and develop strong, lasting relationships. She is also a Registered Clinical Counselor, working with individuals, couples, and families to help them navigate life's challenges and increase their resilience. Deena has a Master's in Education (Counseling Psychology) from the University of Manitoba, a Post-Master's in Family Therapy from the University of Pennsylvania and the Philadelphia Child Guidance Clinic, and is a graduate of the Family Enterprise Advising Program at the UBC Sauder School of Business. She is based in Vancouver, Canada.

deenachochinov.com